Write it in SPANISH

By
CHRISTOPHER KENDRIS
B.S., M.S., Columbia University
in the City of New York
M.A., Ph.D., Northwestern University
in Evanston, Illinois

Formerly Assistant Professor
Department of French and Spanish
State University of New York
Albany, New York

BARRON'S EDUCATIONAL SERIES, INC.

With love
For my three grandsons
Alexander Bryan, Daniel Patrick Christopher,
and Matthew David

All inquiries should be addressed to:
Barron's Educational Series, Inc.
250 Wireless Boulevard
Hauppauge, New York 11788

Library of Congress Catalog Card No. 90-1278
International Standard Book No. 4359-6

Library of Congress Cataloging in Publication Data
Kendris, Christopher.
  Write it in Spanish / by Christopher Kendris.
    p.   cm.
  "Adapted from Beginning to Write in Spanish" —
T.p. verso.
  ISBN 0-8120-4359-6
  1. Spanish language — Textbooks for foreign speakers —
English. 2. Spanish language — Self-instruction.   I. Kendris,
Christopher. Beginning to Write in Spanish.   II. Title.
PC4128.K46 1990
468.2'421 — dc20   90-1278
                                                    CIP

PRINTED IN THE UNITED STATES OF AMERICA

510 98

Contents

About the author v
Introduction vi

TAREA 1 1
¿Quién es?

TAREA 2 3
Las cuatro estaciones del año

TAREA 3 5
Me gusta escribir en español

REVIEW TEST 1 7

TAREA 4 9
¿Cómo está Ud.?

TAREA 5 11
Tengo hambre y tengo sed

TAREA 6 13
Voy al parque

REVIEW TEST 2 15

TAREA 7 17
¿Qué hora es?

TAREA 8 19
¿Dónde está?

TAREA 9 21
Yo leo, contesto y hablo

REVIEW TEST 3 23

TAREA 10 25
Escribo una tarjeta postal

TAREA 11 29
Mi casa

TAREA 12 31
Yo me lavo y me visto

REVIEW TEST 4 33

TAREA 13 35
Yo voy a hacer un viaje

TAREA 14 37
Tengo mucho frío

TAREA 15 39
Doy un paseo

REVIEW TEST 5 41

TAREA 16 43
Nosotros cantamos y comemos

TAREA 17 45
Tengo dolor de cabeza

TAREA 18 47
Estudio español

REVIEW TEST 6 49

TAREA 19 51
Yo voy al cine

TAREA 20 53
Pablo no habla a nadie

TAREA 21 55
Comenzamos a escribir en español

REVIEW TEST 7 57

TAREA 22 59
Mi padre acaba de salir de casa

TAREA 23 61
Yo fui al circo

TAREA 24 63
¿De quién es esta corbata?

REVIEW TEST 8 65

TAREA 25 67
La semana pasada

TAREA 26 69
Ayer yo asistí a una boda

TAREA 27 71
Tengo miedo de cruzar el parque de noche

REVIEW TEST 9 73

TAREA 28 75
Trabajo de más en más

TAREA 29 77
¿Qué pasó?

TAREA 30 79
Fui de compras

REVIEW TEST 10 81

TAREA 31 83
Fui a buscar un regalo

TAREA 32 . . . . **85**
Una señora salió de una panadería

TAREA 33 . . . . **87**
La chica se puso el nuevo sombrero de su madre

REVIEW TEST 11 . . . . **89**

TAREA 34 . . . . **91**
Fui a la ópera anoche

TAREA 35 . . . . **93**
Pienso en este poema

TAREA 36 . . . . **95**
Estoy bastante bien, gracias

REVIEW TEST 12 . . . . **97**

TAREA 37 . . . . **99**
Me alegro mucho de hacer un viaje

TAREA 38 . . . . **101**
Comí un poco de arroz con pollo

TAREA 39 . . . . **103**
Mi padre

TAREA 40 . . . . **105**
¿Cómo se dice en español *I love you?*

REVIEW TEST 13 . . . . **107**

Appendix

◆

Optional situations for conversational and writing skills as enrichment **111**

Antonyms and Synonyms **112**

Review of basic Spanish idioms with **dar & darse, estar, hacer & hacerse, ser, tener** . . **119**

Twenty-two Spanish verbs fully conjugated in all the tenses that you need to use
  in this book **121**

Verbs used in this book **144**

Numbers **145**

Index of idioms, verbal expressions, proverbs and key words showing their location
  in this book **147**

Abbreviations **149**

Vocabulary: Spanish and English words in one alphabetical listing **150**

Answers to all exercises **161**

About the author

◆

Christopher Kendris has worked as interpreter and translator for the U.S. State Department at the American Embassy in Paris.

Dr. Kendris earned his B.S. and M.S. degrees at Columbia University in the City of New York, where he held a New York State scholarship, and his M.A. and Ph. D. degrees at Northwestern University in Evanston, Illinois. He also earned two diplomas with *Mention très Honorable* at the Université de Paris (en Sorbonne), Faculté des Lettres, Ecole Supérieure de Préparation et de Perfectionnement des Professeurs de Français à l'Etranger, and at the Institut de Phonétique, Paris.

He has taught French at the College of The University of Chicago as visiting summer lecturer and at Northwestern University, where he held a Teaching Assistantship and Tutorial Fellowship for four years. He has also taught at Colby College, Duke University, Rutgers—The State University of New Jersey, and the State University of New York at Albany. He was Chairman of the Foreign Languages Department at Farmingdale High School, Farmingdale, New York, where he was also a teacher of French and Spanish.

He is the author of numerous modern language books and workbooks published by Barron's Educational Series, Inc., including *301* and *501 French Verbs, 301* and *501 Spanish Verbs, French Now* (a Level One worktext), *Spanish Now, Book II,* and *How to Prepare for the College Board Achievement Test in French* and *Spanish, French the Easy Way,* and *Spanish the Easy Way.*

In 1986 he was one of ninety-five American high school teachers of foreign languages across the United States who was honored with a Rockefeller Foundation Fellowship in a competition that included about 1,000 candidates. The Fellowship gave him the opportunity to study new teaching methods and techniques at the Pedagogical Institute at the International School of French Language and Civilization at the Alliance Française in Paris. He was one of only four winners in New York State.

Dr. Christopher Kendris is listed in *Contemporary Authors.*

Introduction

◆

This book contains new techniques and exercises to help you improve your skill in writing Spanish simply. If you use this book with a desire to practice, from the first page to the last, you will be able to raise your level of competence from basic to superior provided, of course, that you have some elementary knowledge of the Spanish language.

What I kept in mind constantly while writing this book is your need to get a higher score on the writing sections of standardized exams like the New York State Regents exams and the Second Language Proficiency exams that test your skill in writing simple Spanish.

There are forty assignments in this book. Each one consists of five idioms, expressions, or words that are at the New York State Regents level of competence. Each assignment is related in thought so that a situation or image is created. This arrangement makes it interesting for you and makes it easier to retain the vocabulary in each topic. After every three assignments there is a review test, except for the last test, which covers the last four units. The idioms, expressions, and words have been numbered consecutively for convenience in referring to them.

At the end of this book there are several sections that contain basic review material. Take a few minutes right now to browse through the Table of Contents and the Appendix. I am sure you will find a lot of useful material to review or to learn for the first time.

Here are some highlights in this new book.

1. Each *tarea* is on a topic people enjoy talking or writing about.

2. Practical situations are put into action so they become meaningful.

3. You will have a chance to write lists of words or expressions in Spanish for grocery and shopping lists, things that you would take with you on vacation, telephone messages, and many other situations. You need this kind of practice to write in Spanish because the new Second Language Proficiency exams require you to do the same.

4. The personal topics will motivate you to write about yourself or someone else and to list words to describe yourself or other persons.

5. There are situations where you will have to write a few words in Spanish to persuade someone, to get and give information, to socialize, or to write simple notes or post cards to friends.

6. The Spanish idiomatic expressions, verbs, and words in this book are used all the time in daily life. Whatever you want to say, here is your chance to write it in Spanish! There are also drawings that give you an opportunity to write a few words about them in Spanish.

7. The writing exercises are designed in such a way as to get you to express your feelings with confidence and power in every written word. They will motivate you to open up your thoughts and write them in simple Spanish. As long as you make yourself understood, that is what is important. After all, language is communication when you hear it, speak it, or write it.

8. The Appendix in the back pages of the book contains sections on antonyms and synonyms, a review of basic vocabulary by topics, a review of basic French idioms, and other features that will help you to do your best when you want to write something simple in French.

9. Finally, I have included twenty-two basic Spanish verbs fully conjugated in all the tenses because you will have to refer to that section from time to time when you are writing in Spanish.

I sincerely hope that you get a lot out of this book and that you enjoy using it as much as I enjoyed writing it for you. But, remember, you will get out of this book whatever you put into it. Now, let's begin! Write it in Spanish!

Christopher Kendris
B.S., M.S., M.A., Ph.D.

Me llamo _____
(My name is)

Hoy es _____
(Today is)

(lunes, martes, miércoles, jueves, viernes, sábado, domingo)
(Monday, Tuesday, Wednesday, Thursday, Friday, Saturday, Sunday)

el _____ **de** _____
(primero, dos, tres, *etc.***)** **(septiembre, octubre,** *etc.***)**
(first, second, third, *etc.*) (September, October, *etc.*)

¿Quién es?
(Who is it?)

I. Write a brief sentence of your own in Spanish using the expression given. If you are not ready to do that, just copy the model sentence for practice.

1. **llamarse** to be named, called **Me llamo . . .**
My name is . . .

_____

2. **tener . . . años** to be . . . years old **Tengo diez y siete años.**
I am seventeen years old.

_____

3. **levantarse** to get up **Me levanto a las seis de la mañana.**
I get up at six in the morning.

_____

4. **todas las mañanas** every morning **Todas las mañanas tomo un buen desayuno.**
Every morning I have a good breakfast.

_____

5. **dar a** to look out on, to face **El comedor da al jardín.**
The dining room faces the garden.

_____

II. On the line write in Spanish one word that will make the sentence meaningful and grammatically correct. Refer to the model sentences in Exercise **I** above if you need to.

1. **Me** _____ **Juan.**

2. **Tengo diez y siete** _____.

3. **Me** _____ **a las seis de la mañana.**

4. **Todas las** _____ **tomo un buen desayuno.**

5. **El comedor** _____ **al jardín.**

III. Answer the following questions in Spanish in complete sentences.

1. **¿Cómo se llama Ud.?** _____

_____

2. **¿Cuántos años tiene Ud.?** _____

_____

3. **¿A qué hora se levanta Ud. todas las mañanas?** _____

_____

IV. Write at least three sentences in Spanish about yourself. Refer to Exercises **I, II, III** above.

_____

_____

_____

_____

V. On the line write in Spanish what the person is doing.

¿Qué hace él?
(What is he doing?)

El muchacho bebe leche.

¿Qué hace él?

_____

VI. Change one letter in any part of the word and get another Spanish word.
Example: **como** (how, as)   Change **c** to **t** and you get: **tomo** (I take)

voy   (I'm going) _____ (today)

VII. Add one letter in any part of the word and get another Spanish word.

hora   (hour) _____ (now)

VIII. Write three words in Spanish that are things you eat or drink for breakfast.

1. _____ 2. _____ 3. _____

IX. How many Spanish words can you find in the word **DESAYUNO?** Write at least three.

D E S A Y U N O

1. _____ 2. _____ 3. _____

X. Write two verbs in Spanish stating what you do. They are in this lesson.

1. *Yo* _____ 2. *Yo* _____

Me llamo _____

Hoy es _____

el _____ de _____

Las cuatro estaciones del año

(The four seasons of the year)

I.   Write a brief sentence of your own in Spanish using the expression given. If you are not ready to do that, just copy the model sentence for practice.

6. **hacer calor**   to be warm (weather)   **Hace calor en el verano.**
It is warm in summer.

_____

7. **hacer frío**   to be cold (weather)   **Hace frío en el invierno.**
It is cold in winter.

_____

8. **hacer buen tiempo**   to be good (weather)   **Hace buen tiempo aquí en la primavera.**
The weather is good here in the spring.

_____

9. **hacer fresco**   to be cool (weather)   **Hace fresco aquí en el otoño.**
It is cool here in autumn.

_____

10. **hacer un tiempo agradable**   to be nice (weather)   **Hace un tiempo agradable. Voy al parque.**
It's nice weather. I'm going to the park.

_____

II.   On the line write in Spanish one word that will make the sentence meaningful and grammatically correct. Refer to the model sentences in Exercise **I** above if you need to.

1. **Hace _____ en el verano.**

2. **Hace _____ en el invierno.**

3. **Hace buen _____ aquí en la primavera.**

4. **Hace _____ aquí en el otoño.**

5. **Hace un tiempo _____ . Voy al parque.**

> **MNEMONIC TIP**
> If you still don't know the difference in meaning between **VERANO** (summer) and **INVIERNO** (winter), associate the **IN** spelling like this:
>
> W I N T E R
> I N V I E R N O

III.   Answer the following questions in Spanish in complete sentences.

1. **¿Qué tiempo hace en el verano?** _____

_____

2. ¿Qué tiempo hace en el invierno? _____

_____

3. ¿Qué tiempo hace en la primavera? _____

_____

4. ¿Qué tiempo hace aquí en el otoño? _____

_____

5. ¿Qué tiempo hace hoy? ¿Adónde va Ud.? _____

_____

IV. Write six sentences in Spanish. Tell what the weather is like in autumn, in winter, in the spring and in summer. Also tell what the weather is like today and where you are going. Refer to Exercises **I, II** and **III** above.

_____

_____

_____

_____

_____

_____

V. On the line write in Spanish what the person is doing.

¿Qué hace ella?   La muchacha baila.
(What is she doing?)

¿Qué hace ella?

_____

VI. Change one letter in any part of the word and get another Spanish word.

bien (well) Change this word to: _____ (good)

VII. Add one letter in any part of the word and get another Spanish word.

pero (but) Change this word to: _____ (dog)

VIII. Write six words in Spanish pertaining to the weather.

1. _____   3. _____   5. _____

2. _____   4. _____   6. _____

IX. How many Spanish words can you find in the word **AGRADABLE?** Write at least six.

| A G R A D A B L E |

1. _____   3. _____   5. _____

2. _____   4. _____   6. _____

X. Write one Spanish word to complete the thought in the following sentence.

Voy al parque porque _____ **un tiempo agradable.**

TAREA

3

Me gusta escribir en español.
(I like to write in Spanish.)

I.   Write a brief sentence of your own in Spanish using the expression given. If you are not ready to do that, just copy the model sentence for practice.

11. **llover**   to rain   **Cuando llueve leo un libro en mi dormitorio.**
When it rains I read a book in my room.

_____

12. **nevar**   to snow   **Cuando nieva voy al parque.**
When it snows I go to the park.

_____

13. **dar un paseo**   to take a walk   **Cuando hace buen tiempo doy un paseo en el parque.**
When the weather is good I take a walk in the park.

_____

14. **en casa**   at home   **Leo los periódicos en casa cuando no hace buen tiempo.**
I read the newspapers at home when the weather is not good.

_____

15. **hay (hace) sol** the sun is shining **Cuando hay sol, estoy muy contento.**
When the sun is shining, I'm very happy.

_____

II. On the line write in Spanish one word that will make the sentence meaningful and grammatically correct. Refer to the model sentences in Exercise I above if you need to.

1. **Cuando _____ leo un libro en mi dormitorio.**

2. **Cuando _____ voy al parque.**

3. **Cuando hace buen tiempo _____ un paseo en el parque.**

4. **Leo los periódicos _____ casa cuando no hace buen tiempo.**

5. **Cuando _____ sol, estoy muy contento.**

III. Answer the following questions in Spanish in complete sentences.

1. ¿Qué hace Ud. cuando llueve? _____

_____

2. ¿Qué hace Ud. cuando nieva? _____

_____

3. ¿Qué hace Ud. cuando hace buen tiempo? _____

_____

4. ¿Qué hace Ud. cuando no hace buen tiempo? _____

_____

5. ¿Cuáles son las estaciones del año? _____

_____

IV. Write three sentences in Spanish telling what you do when it rains, what you do when it snows and what you do in a park. Refer to Exercises **I**, **II** and **III** above.

_____

_____

_____

V. On the line write in Spanish what the person is doing.

¿**Qué hace él?**
(What is he doing?)

El muchacho lee un libro.

¿Qué hace él?

_____

VI. Change one letter in any part of the word and get another Spanish word.

cosa (thing) _____ (house)

VII. Change one letter in any part of the word and get another Spanish word.

parque (park) _____ (because)

VIII. Write three verbs in the present indicative tense using **yo** as the subject. They must pertain to three things that you do.

1. _____ 2. _____ 3. _____

IX. The words in the following sentence are scrambled. Write them in the correct word order.

Cuando / parque / al / voy / nieva. _____

X. Write two Spanish words to complete the thought in the following sentence.

Cuando llueve _____ **un libro en** _____ **dormitorio.**

Me llamo _____

Hoy es _____

el _____ **de** _____

I.   Write at least four sentences in Spanish about yourself.

_____

_____

_____

_____

II.   Write at least four sentences in Spanish about the seasons of the year.

_____

_____

_____

_____

III.   Write three sentences in Spanish telling what you do when it rains, what you do when it snows and what you do in a park.

_____

_____

_____

_____

IV.   Complete the following sentences by writing in Spanish words that will make the statements meaningful.

1. **Yo me** _____ **a las seis de la mañana.**

2. **Todas las** _____ **tomo un** _____ **desayuno.**

3. **Hace** _____ **en el invierno y hace calor en el** _____.

4. **Me gusta** _____ **en español.**

V.   You are going shopping. In Spanish, write a list of things you plan to buy.

1. _____   2. _____   3. _____

VI. On the line write in Spanish what the person is doing.

1.

¿Qué hace él?

_____

2.

¿Qué hace ella?

_____

3.

¿Qué hace él?

_____

VII. Change one letter in any part of the word and get another Spanish word.

cosa (thing) _____ (house)

VIII. Change one letter in any part of the word and get another Spanish word.

parque (park) _____ (because)

IX. Write three verbs in the present indicative tense using **yo** as the subject. They must pertain to three things that you do.

1. _____ 2. _____ 3. _____

X. How many Spanish words can you find in the word **AGRADABLE?** Write at least six.

> | A G R A D A B L E |

1. _____ 3. _____ 5. _____

2. _____ 4. _____ 6. _____

Refrán (Proverb) **Tal padre, tal hijo.** Like father, like son.

TAREA

4

¿Cómo está Ud.?

(How are you?)

I. Write a brief sentence of your own in Spanish using the expression given. If you are not ready to do that, just copy the model sentence for practice.

16. **estar bien**   to be (feel) well

¿Está Ud. bien hoy?
Are you feeling well today?

_____

17. **estar enfermo(a)**   to be (feel) ill, sick

No. Estoy enfermo(a). ¿Y Ud.?
No. I feel ill. And you?

_____

18. **estar mejor**   to be (feel) better

Estoy mucho mejor esta mañana, gracias.
I feel much better this morning, thank you.

_____

19. **al campo**   to the country

¿Va Ud. al campo este año?
Are you going to the country this year?

_____

20. **pasar una semana**   to spend a week

Sí. Voy a pasar una semana en el campo.
Yes. I'm going to spend a week in the country.

_____

II. On the line write in Spanish one word that will make the sentence meaningful and grammatically correct.

1. **¿Está Ud. _____ hoy?**

2. **No. Yo _____ enfermo(a). ¿Y Ud.?**

3. **Estoy mucho _____ esta mañana, gracias.**

4. **¿Va Ud. _____ campo este año?**

5. **Sí. Voy a _____ una semana en el campo.**

III. Answer the following questions in Spanish in complete sentences.

1. **¿Cómo está Ud.?** _____

2. **¿Cómo está su amigo?** _____

3. **¿Qué hace Ud. cuando está enfermo(a)?** _____

_____

4. **¿Adónde va Ud. a pasar dos semanas este año?** _____

_____

5. **¿Adónde va Ud. ahora?** _____

IV.   List six words in Spanish that you would use when talking about how you feel.

1. _____   3. _____   5. _____

2. _____   4. _____   6. _____

V.   On the line write in Spanish what the persons are doing.

¿Qué hacen ellos?   **La chica y el chico corren.**
(What are they doing?)

¿Qué hacen ellos?

_____

VI.   Write three adverbs in Spanish that would describe how you feel.

1. _____   2. _____   3. _____

VII.   A friend has asked you where you are going to spend one week this summer. On the line, write in Spanish where you plan to go.

_____

VIII.   A friend has asked you how many weeks you are going to spend in the country. On the line, write in Spanish either one week or two weeks.

_____

IX.   Write three words in Spanish naming things you would take with you when you spend two weeks in the country.

1. _____   2. _____   3. _____

X.   Write a note to a friend of yours saying that you are going to spend one week in the country. Also tell your friend that you are leaving tomorrow. Begin your note with **Querido amigo** if it is a boy or **Querida amiga** if it is a girl. End the note with **Hasta la vista.** Then write your name.

_____

_____

_____

_____

XI.   **Diálogo.** Write Spanish words on the lines to complete the thought. It is a conversation between you and a doctor.

El médico: **Buenos días. ¿Está Ud. _____ hoy?**

Usted: **No, señor. Estoy _____.**

El médico: **¿Cuántos años tiene Ud.?**

Usted: **Tengo _____ años.**

El médico: **Tome este medicamento _____ las mañanas.**

Usted: **Sí, doctor. Muchas gracias.**

Tengo hambre y tengo sed.

(I'm hungry and I'm thirsty.)

I. Write a brief sentence of your own in Spanish using the expression given. If you are not ready to do that, just copy the model sentence for practice.

21.	**tener ganas de (+ inf.)**	to feel like (+ pres. part.)	**Tengo ganas de comer.** I feel like eating.

_____

22.	**tener hambre**	to be hungry	**Como cuando tengo hambre.** I eat when I'm hungry.

_____

23.	**tener sed**	to be thirsty	**Bebo agua cuando tengo sed.** I drink water when I'm thirsty.

_____

24.	**acostumbrar (+ inf.)**	to be in the habit of (+ pres. part.)	**Acostumbro comer temprano.** I'm in the habit of eating early.

_____

25.	**entrar en (+ noun)**	to enter (into a place), go in	**Entro en el restaurante para comer.** I'm going into the restaurant to eat.

_____

II. On the line write in Spanish one word that will make the sentence meaningful and grammatically correct.

1. **Tengo ganas _____ comer.**

2. **Como cuando _____ hambre.**

3. **Bebo agua cuando tengo _____ .**

4. **Acostumbro _____ temprano.**

5. **Entro _____ el restaurante para comer.**

III. Answer the following questions in Spanish in complete sentences.

1. **¿Tiene Ud. ganas de comer o beber?** _____

_____

2. **¿Qué hace Ud. cuando tiene hambre?** _____

_____

3. ¿Qué hace Ud. cuando tiene sed? _____

_____

4. ¿Acostumbra Ud. comer en casa o en un restaurante? _____

_____

5. ¿Para qué entra una persona en un restaurante? _____

_____

IV. Look at the picture and study the statements in Spanish. Then, on the lines, write answers in Spanish to the questions.

1. **¿Qué es esto?**	2. **¿Es un sombrero?**	3. **No es un sombrero.**
(What is this?)	(Is it a hat?)	(It is not a hat.)
4. **Es un bizcocho.**	5. **¿Es delicioso?**	6. **Sí, es delicioso.**
(It's a cake.)	(Is it delicious?)	(Yes, it's delicious.)

Complete the answers in Spanish.

1. **¿Qué es esto? ¿Es un sombrero?**

   No _____. *Es* _____.

2. **¿Es delicioso?** *Sí,* _____.

V. You are going to a supermarket. Write a short grocery list. Use Spanish words in this lesson and in previous ones. You may also look up words in the vocabulary pages in the back of this book.

1. _____ 2. _____ 3. _____

4. _____ 5. _____ 6. _____

VI. Answer the following questions in Spanish.

1. **¿Cuándo come Ud.?** _____

2. **¿Cuándo bebe Ud.?** _____

3. **¿Dónde acostumbra Ud. comer?** _____

_____

VII. A friend of yours has asked you to have dinner in a restaurant. You refuse politely and you give one reason for not accepting the invitation. Write your response in Spanish on the line.

_____

Voy al parque.

(I'm going to the park.)

I. Write a brief sentence of your own in Spanish using the expression given. If you are not ready to do that, just copy the model sentence for practice.

26. **hay**   there is, there are   **Hay un gran parque en esta ciudad.**
There is a big park in this city.

_____

27. **me gusta (+ inf.)**   I like to (+ inf.)   **Me gusta jugar en el parque.**
I like to play in the park.

_____

28. **cerca de**   near   **El parque está cerca de mi casa.**
The park is (located) near my house.

_____

29. **jugar al tenis**   to play tennis   **Me gusta jugar al tenis en el parque.**
I like to play tennis in the park.

_____

30. **jugar a la pelota**   to play ball   **Ahora voy a jugar a la pelota en el parque.**
Now I'm going to play ball in the park.

_____

II. On the line write in Spanish one word that will make the sentence meaningful and grammatically correct.

1. **Hay un** _____ **parque en esta ciudad.**

2. **Me** _____ **jugar en el parque.**

3. **El parque** _____ **cerca de mi casa.**

4. **Me gusta** _____ **al tenis en el parque.**

5. **Ahora voy a jugar a la** _____ **en el parque.**

III. Write Spanish words to complete the paragraph. The words you need are in this lesson.

Hay un gran parque en _____ **ciudad. Me gusta** _____ **en el parque. El**

parque _____ **cerca** _____ **mi casa. Me gusta jugar** _____ **tenis en el**

parque. Ahora yo _____ **a** _____ **a la** _____ **en el parque.**

IV. Answer the following questions in Spanish in complete sentences.

1. **¿Cuántos parques hay en esta ciudad?** _____

_____

2. **¿Cuándo va Ud. al parque?** _____

_____

3. **¿Dónde está el parque?** _____

_____

4. **¿Qué le gusta a Ud. hacer en el parque?** _____

_____

5. **¿Adónde va Ud. hoy?** _____

_____

V. On the lines write in Spanish where the girl is and what she is doing.

**La muchacha está
en un parque.**

¿Dónde está ella?

Ella _____

**Ella juega a la
pelota.**

¿Qué hace ella?

Ella _____

VI. A friend of yours asks you where you are going. Tell him or her that you are going to the park. You may give your own reason for going there or you may want to say that you are going to play ball or tennis. Write your response on the line.

_____

VII. **Diálogo.** You and a friend are talking about playing in the park. On the lines write Spanish words to complete the thought. Use the vocabulary in this lesson or in the back pages of this book for words you do not know.

Tu amigo(a):   **¿Adónde vas?**

Tú: **Yo _____ al parque.**

Tu amigo(a):   **¿Por qué?**

Tú: **Para _____ .**

Tu amigo(a):   **¿Para jugar a la pelota?**

Tú: **No. Para jugar _____ .**

Me llamo ____________________

Hoy es ____________________

el ____________ de ____________

REVIEW TEST

2

TAREAS 4, 5, 6

I. Write a short paragraph in Spanish. Write that you are not feeling well today, that you are going to the country, and that you are going to spend two weeks there.

II. Write a short paragraph in Spanish. Tell what you feel like doing now, what you do when you are hungry, what you do when you are thirsty, and where you are in the habit of eating.

III. Write a short paragraph in Spanish. Tell where there is a park and how you get to the park. Also, mention two things that you like to do in a park and when you go there.

IV. Look at the pictures and answer the questions in Spanish.

1.
¿Qué hacen la chica y el chico?

_____

2.
¿Qué es esto?

_____

3.
¿Qué hace la muchacha?

_____

Refrán   (Proverb)   **Dicho y hecho.**   No sooner said than done.

TAREA

7

¿Qué hora es?

(What time is it?)

I. Write a brief sentence of your own in Spanish using the expression given. If you are not ready to do that, just copy the model sentence for practice.

31. **¿Qué hora es?**   What time is it?   **¿Qué hora es?**
What time is it?

_____

32. **Es la una.**   It is one o'clock.   **Es la una. No, perdóneme. Son las dos.**
    Son las dos.   It is two o'clock.   It is one o'clock. No, excuse me. It is two o'clock.

_____

33. **a qué hora . . .**   at what time . . .   **¿A qué hora va Ud. a la clase de español?**
At what time are you going to Spanish class?

_____

34. **a las tres**   at three o'clock   **Voy a la clase de español a las tres.**
I'm going to Spanish class at three o'clock.

_____

35. **tener cita**   to have an appointment   **Yo tengo cita con el dentista a las dos y media.**
I have an appointment with the dentist at two thirty.

_____

II. On the line write in Spanish one word that will make the sentence meaningful and grammatically correct.

1. **¿Qué hora _____?**

2. **Es la _____.**

3. **Son _____ dos.**

4. **¿A _____ hora va Ud. a la clase de español?**

5. **Voy a la clase de español a las _____.**

6. **Yo _____ cita con el dentista a las dos y media.**

III. Answer the following questions in Spanish.

1. **¿Qué hora es, por favor?** _____

_____

2. ¿A qué hora toma Ud. el desayuno? _____

_____

3. ¿A qué hora toma Ud. el almuerzo? _____

_____

4. ¿A qué hora toma Ud. la cena? _____

_____

5. ¿A qué hora se acuesta Ud. todas las noches? _____

_____

IV. Write Spanish words to complete the paragraph. The words you need are in this lesson. Read the paragraph at least one time before you write Spanish words.

Es _____ una. No, perdóneme. Son _____ dos. Yo _____ a

_____ clase _____ español a _____ tres. Yo _____ cita

_____ el dentista _____ las dos _____ media.

V. On the lines under the clocks write in Spanish the time that is given.

1.

2.

_____   _____

VI. A friend of yours asks you at what time you are going to Spanish class. Tell him or her that you are going to Spanish class at three o'clock. Then tell your friend that you have an appointment with the dentist at four o'clock.

_____

_____

VII. Write a list of places you have to go at a certain hour. For example, you are going to Spanish class at one o'clock, you are going to the dentist at three o'clock, and you are going home at four o'clock. Or, you may state other places where you are going and at other times.

1. _____

2. _____

3. _____

VIII. You are working in a dentist's office. You answer a telephone call from Señora García. She would like you to take a message saying that she has an appointment with the dentist at three o'clock but she is arriving at four o'clock. On the lines, write the phone message in Spanish.

La fecha _____

La hora _____

_____

_____

Su nombre _____

¿Dónde está?

(Where is it?)

I. Write a brief sentence of your own in Spanish using the expression given. If you are not ready to do that, just copy the model sentence for practice.

36. **Aquí tiene Ud. . . .**	here you have, here is. . .	**¡Aquí tiene Ud. un museo! Hay muchas obras de arte en un museo.** Here is a museum! There are many art objects in a museum.	

_____

37. **Ahí tiene Ud. . .**	there you have, there is. . .	**¡Ahí tiene Ud. la biblioteca! Hay muchos libros en una biblioteca.** There is the library! There are many books in a library.

_____

38. **a la derecha**	to (on) the right	**La estación del ferrocarril está a la derecha.** The railroad station is on the right.

_____

39. **a la izquierda**	to (on) the left	**La escuela está a la izquierda.** The school is on the left.

_____

40. **hay que (+ inf.)**	it is necessary (+ inf.), one must	**Hay que tomar el autobús para llegar a la universidad.** It's necessary to take the bus to get to the university.

_____

II. On the line write in Spanish one word that will make the sentence meaningful and grammatically correct.

1. **¡Aquí _____ Ud. un museo!**

2. **Hay muchas obras de arte en un _____.**

3. **¡Ahí _____ Ud. la biblioteca!**

4. **Hay _____ libros en una biblioteca.**

5. **La estación _____ a la derecha.**

6. **La escuela está a la _____.**

III. Answer the following questions in Spanish. You may write a complete sentence or only two or three words. Your answers must show that you understood the questions. What you write must be comprehensible.

1. **¿Qué hay en un museo?** _____

_____

2. **¿Qué hay en una biblioteca?** _____

_____

3. **¿Dónde está la estación del ferrocarril?** _____

_____

4. **¿A qué hora se acuesta Ud. todas las noches?** _____

_____

5. **¿Le gusta a Ud. escribir en español?** _____

_____

IV. On the lines write in Spanish what there is in the places indicated.

1. In a museum _____

2. In a library _____

V. Here is a Spanish train ticket. Examine it carefully. Answer the questions in Spanish in just a few words.

BILLETE DE TREN		Clase **2**
Origen MADRID—Estación Goya		
Destino BARCELONA—Estación Norte		
Valedero del 22 de octubre al 21 de diciembre		

Adultos	002	**Animales** 000	**Precio** 501 Pesetas
Niños	003	**Reducción de precio** 000	**Número del billete** 8972900

1. **¿Cuántas pesetas cuesta este billete?** _____

2. **¿De qué ciudad sale Ud.?** _____

3. **¿A qué ciudad va Ud.?** _____

4. **¿A qué estación llega Ud.?** _____

5. **¿En qué clase viaja Ud.?** _____

6. **¿Este billete es para cuántos adultos?** _____

   ¿Cuántos niños? _____

7. **¿Este billete es valedero de qué fecha hasta qué fecha?** _____

8. **¿Hay una reducción de precio?** _____

Me llamo _____

Hoy es _____

el _____ de _____

Yo leo, contesto y hablo.

(I read, I answer, and I talk.)

I. Write a brief sentence of your own in Spanish using the expression given. If you are not ready to do that, just copy the model sentence for practice.

41. **¡Vamos a ver!**   Let's see!   **¡Vamos a ver! ¿Quién va a leer?**
Let's see! Who is going to read?

_____

42. **tocarle a uno**   to be someone's turn   **Le toca a Roberto.**
It's Robert's turn.

_____

43. **saber (+ inf.)**   to know how (+ inf.)   **Roberto sabe leer muy bien en inglés.**
Robert knows how to read English very well.

_____

44. **en voz alta**   in a loud voice, aloud   **Roberto habla en voz alta.**
Robert speaks in a loud voice.

_____

45. **en voz baja**   in a soft (low) voice   **Yo contesto siempre en voz baja.**
I always answer in a soft voice.

_____

II. On the line write in Spanish one word that will make the sentence meaningful and grammatically correct.

1. **¡Vamos _____ ver! ¿Quién va a leer?**

2. **Le toca _____ Roberto.**

3. **Roberto sabe _____ muy bien en inglés.**

4. **Roberto habla en _____ alta.**

5. **Yo contesto siempre en voz _____.**

III. Answer the following questions in Spanish. You may write a complete sentence or only two or three words. Your answers must show that you understood the questions. What you write must be comprehensible.

1. **¿Le gusta a Ud. leer en español?** _____

_____

2. **¿A quién le toca leer?** _____

_____

3. **¿En qué lengua sabe Ud. escribir?** _____

_____

4. **¿Habla Ud. en voz alta o en voz baja?** _____

_____

5. **¿A qué hora almuerza usted?** _____

_____

IV. On the lines write in Spanish an antonym (opposite meaning) for each of the following. Refer to words in this lesson and to previous ones. See Antonyms in the Appendix.

1. **en voz baja** _____ 3. **a la derecha** _____

2. **bien** _____ 4. **estar enfermo(a)** _____

V. **Diálogo.** Write Spanish words on the lines to complete the dialogue. It is a conversation between you and Roberto about reading and talking.

Roberto: **¿Quién va a leer?**

Tú: _____

Roberto: **¿Sabes leer muy bien en español?**

Tú: _____

Roberto: **¿Hablas en voz alta o en voz baja en la clase de español?**

Tú: _____

VI. The following letters are scrambled. Place them in the correct order to form a Spanish word. They are all in this lesson.

1. **R E E L** _____   4. **A L O H B** _____

2. **B L A H A R** _____   5. **O E L** _____

3. **O T S C E N T O** _____   6. **I M P R S E E** _____

VII.

¿Qué es esto?

Es _____.

Me llamo _____

Hoy es _____

el _____ **de** _____

I. Write two sentences in Spanish. Write that you are going to Spanish class at one o'clock and that you have an appointment with the dentist at two thirty.

_____

_____

II. Write a short paragraph in Spanish containing four sentences. Tell what there is in a museum and in a library. Also write that the museum is on the left and the library is on the right.

_____

_____

_____

_____

_____

_____

III. Write a short paragraph in Spanish containing four sentences. Write that Roberto is going to read in English and you are going to read in Spanish. Also write that Elena is going to write in English and you are going to write in Spanish.

_____

_____

_____

_____

_____

_____

IV. Look at the pictures and answer the questions in Spanish.

1. **¿Qué es esto?**

_____

2. ¿Qué hora es?

3. ¿Qué hora es?

_____

_____

BILLETE DE TREN   Clase **2**

Origen	BARCELONA—Estación Norte
Destino	MADRID—Estación Goya
Valedero	del 22 de septiembre al 21 de octubre

Adultos 002	**Animales** 000	**Precio**	501 Pesetas
Niños 003	**Reducción de precio** 000	**Número del billete**	8972900

---

4. **¿Cuántas pesetas cuesta este billete?** _____

_____

5. **¿De qué ciudad sale usted?** _____

_____

6. **¿A qué ciudad va usted?** _____

_____

7. **¿A qué estación llega usted?** _____

_____

8. **¿En qué clase viaja usted?** _____

_____

9. **¿Este billete es para cuántos adultos?** _____

_____

¿Cuántos niños? _____

_____

10. **¿Este billete es valedero de qué fecha hasta qué fecha?** _____

_____

Refrán   **Más vale tarde que nunca.**   Better late than never.

Me llamo _____

Hoy es _____

el _____ de _____

Escribo una tarjeta postal.

(I'm writing a post card.)

I. Write a brief sentence of your own in Spanish using the expression given. If you are not ready to do that, just copy the model sentence for practice.

46. **la semana que viene**   next week   **La semana que viene voy a España.**
Next week I am going to Spain.

_____

_____

_____

47. **pensar (+ inf.)**   to intend, plan, expect (+ inf.)   **Pienso ir a Madrid.**
I intend to go to Madrid.

_____

_____

_____

48. **al (+ inf.)**   on (upon) (+ pres. part.)   **Al llegar a Madrid, pienso ir a un hotel.**
Upon arriving in Madrid, I expect to go to a hotel.

_____

_____

_____

49. **pasearse en automóvil**   to take a ride in a car   **Quiero pasearme en automóvil por las calles de Madrid.**
I want to ride in a car through the streets of Madrid.

_____

_____

_____

50. **ahora mismo**   right now   **Ahora mismo voy a escribir a mi amiga que está en Madrid.**
Right now I'm going to write to my friend who is in Madrid.

_____

_____

_____

II. Write a post card in Spanish to Margarita Morales, your Spanish pen pal. Tell her at least three things about yourself. Refer to the previous lessons if you have to.

Querida Margarita,

_____

_____

_____

_____

_____

_____

_____ .

Con cariño,

_____

Srta. Margarita Morales
15 Avenida Goya
Madrid
España

correo   aéreo

III. Answer the following questions in Spanish. You may write a complete sentence or only two or three words. Your answers must show that you understood the questions. What you write must be comprehensible.

1. **¿Qué piensa hacer Ud. el sábado que viene?** _____

_____

2. **¿Quiere Ud. ir a Madrid? ¿Por qué?** _____

_____

3. **¿Qué hace Ud. generalmente al llegar a su casa?** _____

_____

4. **¿Cómo se llama su mejor amigo(a)?** _____

_____

5. **¿Qué frutas le gustan a Ud.? Mencione tres.** _____

_____

IV. Read the following business letter. Then answer the questions below it. You may write a complete sentence or only two or three words. Your answers must show that you understood the questions. What you write must be comprehensible. Don't forget to use the vocabulary pages in the back of this book.

Lunes, el 22 de noviembre

Señor Miguel Domingo, Director
LA REVISTA DE LENGUAS
465, Avenida de los Reyes
32012 Madrid

Estimado Señor:

Soy estudiante de lenguas. Aprendo inglés, francés, italiano, y alemán en el Colegio de Madrid.

Me gustan mucho las lenguas. Hágame el favor de enviarme un ejemplar de su revista.

Muchas gracias.

Atentamente,

Paula Martínez

Paula Martínez
12, Calle de las Flores
32001 Madrid

1. **¿Cuál es la fecha de la carta?** _____

_____

2. **¿Quién escribe la carta?** _____

_____

3. **¿Qué desea recibir Paula Martínez?** _____

_____

4. **¿Qué lenguas aprende ella?** _____

_____

5. **¿Dónde vive Paula Martínez?** _____

_____

Write the heading in Spanish as you have learned to do in the previous lessons.

TAREA
11

Mi casa
(My house)

I. Write two sentences of your own in Spanish using the expression given. If you are not ready to do that, just copy each model sentence twice for practice.

51. **estar situado(a)**   to be located   **Mi casa está situada cerca de aquí.**
My house is (located) near here.

_____

_____

52. **poner la mesa**   to set the table   **En mi casa mi madre pone la mesa.**
In my house my mother sets the table.

_____

_____

53. **a veces**   at times   **A veces mi hermana pone la mesa.**
At times my sister sets the table.

_____

_____

54. **de vez en cuando**   from time to time   **De vez en cuando yo trabajo en el jardín.**
From time to time I work in the garden.

_____

_____

55. **al lado de**   next door to, beside   **Al lado de nuestra casa hay buenos vecinos.**
Next door to our house there are good neighbors.

_____

_____

II. On the line write in Spanish one word that will make the sentence meaningful and grammatically correct.

1. **Mi casa** _____ **situada cerca de aquí.**

2. **En mi casa mi** _____ **pone la mesa.**

3. **A** _____ **mi hermana pone la mesa.**

4. **De** _____ **en cuando yo trabajo en el jardín.**

5. **Al** _____ **de nuestra casa hay buenos vecinos.**

Mi casa   **29**

III. Answer the following questions in Spanish. You may write a complete sentence or only two or three words. Your answers must show that you understood the questions. What you write must be comprehensible.

1. **¿Dónde está situada su casa?** _____

_____

2. **¿Quién pone la mesa en su casa?** _____

_____

3. **¿Qué hace Ud. en su jardín?** _____

_____

IV. Read the following advertisement. On the lines, write in Spanish three things that sometimes need repair in your house; for example, a faucet, radiator, dryer, and so on. Or, you may want to say in Spanish the plumbing, heating, electricity.

1. _____ 2. _____ 3. _____

S. O. S. SERVICIOS
267, Avenida de los Estados Unidos
32011 Madrid
Tel. 34-45-52-73

● **Fontanería**   ● **Calefacción**

● **Electricidad**

Servicio rápido y excelente—24 horas de servicio
● *día y noche* ●

V. Answer the following questions in Spanish. Don't forget to use the vocabulary pages in the back of this book.

¿Qué es esto?   **¿Qué es esto?**

1. _____   2. _____

Write the heading in Spanish as you have learned to do
in the previous lessons.

_____

_____

Yo me lavo y me visto.

(I wash myself and dress myself.)

I. Write two sentences of your own in Spanish using the expression given. If you are not ready to do that, just copy each model sentence twice for practice.

56. **lavarse**   to wash oneself   **Yo me lavo todas las mañanas.**
I wash myself every morning.

_____

_____

57. **antes de**   before (+ pres.   **Antes de salir de casa, me lavo.**
    (+ inf.)   participle)   Before leaving the house, I wash myself.

_____

_____

58. **limpiarse los**   to brush one's teeth   **Me limpio los dientes todas las mañanas.**
    dientes   I brush my teeth every morning.

_____

_____

59. **vestirse**   to dress oneself   **Me visto en mi dormitorio.**
I dress (myself) in my room.

_____

_____

60. **peinarse**   to comb one's hair   **Me peino todas las mañanas antes de salir de casa.**
I comb my hair every morning before leaving the house.

_____

_____

II. On the line write in Spanish one word that will make the sentence meaningful and grammatically correct.

1. **Yo** _____ **lavo todas las mañanas.**

2. **Antes** _____ **salir de casa, me lavo.**

3. **Me limpio los dientes** _____ **las mañanas.**

4. **Yo me** _____ **en mi dormitorio.**

5. **Yo me** _____ **todas las mañanas antes de salir de casa.**

III. Answer the following questions in Spanish. You may write a complete sentence or only two or three words. Your answers must show that you understood the questions. What you write must be comprehensible. Answers with just **sí** or **no** are not acceptable.

1. **¿Se lava Ud. todas las mañanas?** _____

_____

2. **¿Se lava Ud. antes de salir de casa?** _____

_____

3. **¿Se limpia Ud. los dientes todas las mañanas?** _____

_____

4. **¿Se peina Ud. todos los días?** _____

_____

5. **¿En qué cuarto se viste Ud.?** _____

_____

IV. **Lists.** In the spaces below, write a list of words in Spanish as directed in each situation. They are all in this lesson.

A. Write three verbs in Spanish that you would use to describe the picture.

1. _____ 2. _____ 3. _____

B. Write three nouns in Spanish that you would use to describe the picture.

1. _____ 2. _____ 3. _____

Write the heading in Spanish.

_____

_____

I. Write a post card in Spanish to Margarita Morales, your Spanish pen pal. Tell her at least three things about yourself.

II. Write four sentences in Spanish. Tell where your house is located, who sets the table for meals **(para las comidas),** what you do in the garden from time to time, and a word or two about the neighbors next door.

_____

_____

_____

_____

_____

III. **Lists.** Write four words in Spanish of things in your house that sometimes need to be repaired.

1. _____   3. _____

2. _____   4. _____

IV. On the lines write the missing words in Spanish. They are all in lessons 10, 11, 12.

1. **La** _____ **que viene voy a España.**

2. **Pienso** _____ **a un hotel.**

3. **Yo** _____ **una tarjeta postal.**

4. **Yo** _____ **en el jardín.**

5. **Mi hermana** _____ **la mesa.**

6. **Yo me** _____ **los dientes.**

V. **Diálogo.** Look at the picture below and complete the dialogue by writing one word in Spanish on the lines.

La madre: **Pablo, tú no te** _____ .
①

El chico: **Pero, mamá, yo** _____ **lavo todas las mañanas.**
②

La madre: **Tú no te** _____ **los dientes.**
③

El chico: **Pero yo me lavo** _____ **manos. ¿Tú ves?**
④

Refrán **Más vale pájaro en mano que ciento volando.** A bird in the hand is worth two in the bush.

Write the heading in Spanish as you have learned to do
in the previous lessons.

_____

_____

Yo voy a hacer un viaje.

(I'm going to take a trip.)

I. Write two sentences of your own in Spanish using the expression given. If you are not ready to do that, just copy each model sentence twice for practice.

61. **hacer un viaje**   to take a trip, to go on a trip   **Mañana voy a hacer un viaje con unos amigos míos.**
Tomorrow I'm going to take a trip with some friends of mine.

_____

_____

62. **tener que (+ inf.)**   to have to   **Tengo que hacer los preparativos para el viaje.**
I have to make preparations for the trip.

_____

_____

63. **hacer las maletas**   to pack one's suitcases   **Tengo que hacer las maletas.**
I have to pack my suitcases.

_____

_____

64. **acostarse**   to go to bed   **Tengo que acostarme temprano.**
I have to go to bed early.

_____

_____

65. **de madrugada**   at dawn, at daybreak   **Tengo que levantarme de madrugada.**
I have to get up at daybreak.

_____

_____

II. On the line write in Spanish one word that will make the sentence meaningful and grammatically correct.

1. **Mañana voy a _____ un viaje con unos amigos míos.**

2. **Tengo _____ hacer los preparativos para el viaje.**

3. **Tengo que _____ las maletas.**

4. **Tengo que _____ temprano.**

5. **Tengo que levantarme _____ madrugada.**

III. Answer the following questions in Spanish. You may write a complete sentence or only two or three words. Your answers must show that you understood the questions. What you write must be comprehensible.

1. **¿Cuándo va a hacer usted un viaje?** _____

_____

2. **¿A qué hora tiene Ud. que levantarse mañana?** _____

_____

3. **Mencione Ud. dos cosas que tiene que hacer.** _____

_____

4. **¿Por qué tiene usted que acostarse temprano?** _____

_____

IV. **¿Qué es esto?**   **¿Y qué es esto?**

1. *Es* _____   2. *Es* _____

V. **Lists.** In the spaces below, write a list of words in Spanish as directed in each situation.

A. Write in Spanish two things you will have to do in preparing to take a trip.

1. _____ 2. _____

B. Write three expressions in Spanish, each containing a verb, that you would use when talking about a trip you plan to take.

1. _____ 2. _____ 3. _____

VI. Write a short paragraph in Spanish consisting of at least three sentences saying that you are going on a trip tomorrow, that you must make preparations for the trip, and that you must pack your suitcases, too.

_____

_____

_____

_____

Write the heading in Spanish as you have learned to do
in the previous lessons.

_____

_____

Tengo mucho frío.

(I feel very cold.)

I.   Write two sentences of your own in Spanish using the expression given. If you are not ready to do
      that, just copy each model sentence twice for practice.

66. **Hágame el favor de**   Please (+ verb)   **Hágame el favor de cerrar la ventana.**
    (+ inf.)   Please close the window.

                                                    _____

                                                    _____

67. **¡Cómo no!**   certainly   **¡Cómo no!**
                                                    Certainly!

                                                    _____

                                                    _____

68. **tener frío**   to be (feel) cold   **Tengo mucho frío.**
                                                    I'm very cold.

                                                    _____

                                                    _____

69. **tener calor**   to be (feel) warm   **¿Tiene frío? ¡Yo tengo calor en este cuarto!**
                                                    You feel cold? I feel warm in this room!

                                                    _____

                                                    _____

70. **quitarse**   to take off   **¿Tiene calor? ¡Quítese Ud. la chaqueta!**
                                                    You feel warm? Take off your jacket!

                                                    _____

                                                    _____

II.   On the line write in Spanish one word that will make the sentence meaningful and grammatically
      correct.

   1. **Hágame el _____ de cerrar la ventana.**

   2. **¡Cómo _____!**

   3. **Tengo _____ frío.**

   4. **¿Tiene frío? ¡Yo _____ calor en este cuarto!**

   5. **¿Tiene calor? ¡_____ Ud. la chaqueta!**

III. Answer the following questions in Spanish. You may write a complete sentence or only two or three words. Your answers must show that you understood the questions. What you write must be comprehensible.

1. **¿Qué hace Ud. cuando tiene frío?** _____
   _____

2. **¿Qué hace Ud. cuando tiene calor?** _____
   _____

3. **¿Qué hace Ud. cuando está enfermo(a)?** _____
   _____

4. **¿En qué estación del año hace frío?** _____
   _____

5. **¿En qué estación del año hace calor?** _____
   _____

IV. Look at the picture. Write Spanish words and expressions you would use to talk about the scene.

1. _____ 3. _____

2. _____ 4. _____

Write the heading in Spanish.

_____

_____

Doy un paseo.
(I'm taking a walk.)

I. Write two sentences of your own in Spanish using the expression given. If you are not ready to do that, just copy each model sentence twice for practice.

71. **pasar un buen rato**   to have a good time   **Paso un buen rato todos los sábados.**
I have a good time every Saturday.

_____

_____

72. **gozar de**   to enjoy   **Gozo de las fiestas los sábados.**
I enjoy parties on Saturdays.

_____

_____

73. **dar de comer a**   to feed   **Doy de comer a los pájaros en el parque.**
I feed the birds in the park.

_____

_____

74. **a lo largo de**   along   **Doy un paseo a lo largo de la playa los sábados.**
I take a walk along the beach on Saturdays.

_____

_____

75. **tocar el piano**   to play the piano   **También, me gusta tocar el piano los sábados.**
Also, I like to play the piano on Saturdays.

_____

_____

II. On the line write in Spanish one word that will make the sentence meaningful and grammatically correct.

1. **Paso un _____ rato todos los sábados.**

2. **Gozo _____ las fiestas los sábados.**

3. **Doy _____ comer a los pájaros en el parque.**

4. **Doy un paseo a _____ largo de la playa los sábados.**

5. **También, me gusta _____ el piano los sábados.**

III. Answer the following questions in Spanish. You may write a complete sentence or only two or three words. Your answers must show that you understood the questions. What you write must be comprehensible.

1. **¿Cómo pasa Ud. los sábados?** _____

_____

2. **¿Qué hace Ud. a lo largo de una playa?** _____

_____

3. **¿Por qué estudia Ud. el español?** _____

_____

4. **¿Cuántos días hay en una semana?** _____

_____

5. **¿Cuántas semanas hay en un año?** _____

_____

IV. On the lines write in Spanish what each person is doing.

¿Qué hace él?   **¿Qué hace ella?**

1. _____   2. _____

V. Write a short paragraph in Spanish stating at least five things that you do on Saturdays.

_____

_____

_____

VI. How many Spanish words can you find hidden in the word **INVIERNO?** Find at least four.

> **I N V I E R N O**

1. _____ 2. _____ 3. _____ 4. _____

VII. Change one letter in any part of the word and get another Spanish word. The words are all in this lesson.

Example: **tomo** (I take)   You write: **como** (I eat)

1. **porque** _____   3. **en** _____

2. **voy** _____   4. **plaza** _____

Write the heading in Spanish.

_____

_____

I. **¿Qué es esto?**

1. _____

II. Write a short paragraph in Spanish consisting of at least three sentences saying that you are going on a trip tomorrow, that you must make preparations for the trip, and that you must pack your suitcases, too.

_____

_____

_____

_____

_____

_____

_____

III. Write a short paragraph in Spanish consisting of at least three sentences saying what you do when you feel cold, when you feel warm, and what you do when you feel sick.

_____

_____

_____

_____

_____

_____

_____

_____

IV. Answer the following questions in Spanish. You may write a complete sentence or only two or three words. Your answers must show that you understood the questions. What you write must be comprehensible.

1. **¿Cómo pasa usted los sábados?** _____

_____

2. **¿Qué hace usted a lo largo de una playa?** _____

_____

3. **¿Qué instrumento musical toca usted?** _____

_____

V. **Lists.** In the spaces below, write a list of words or expressions in Spanish as directed in each situation.

A. Write in Spanish two things you will have to do in preparing to take a trip.

1. _____ 2. _____

B. Write three expressions in Spanish, each containing a verb, that you would use when talking about a trip you plan to take.

1. _____ 2. _____ 3. _____

VI. Change one letter in any part of the word and get another Spanish word.

Example: **tomo** (I take)   You write: **como** (I eat)

1. **porque** _____ 3. **en** _____

2. **voy** _____ 4. **plaza** _____

VII. On the line write in Spanish one word that will make the sentence meaningful and grammatically correct.

1. **Mañana yo** _____ **a hacer un viaje con unos amigos míos.**

2. **Tengo** _____ **hacer los preparativos para el** _____ **.**

3. **Yo** _____ **que levantarme de madrugada.**

4. **Hágame el** _____ **de cerrar la ventana.**

5. **Yo tengo calor en este** _____ **.**

6. **Doy de comer a los pájaros en el** _____ **.**

Refrán   **Mucho ruido y pocas nueces.**   Much ado about nothing.

Write the heading in Spanish.

_____

_____

Nosotros cantamos y comemos.

(We sing and we eat.)

I. Write two sentences of your own in Spanish using the expression given. If you are not ready to do that, just copy each model sentence twice for practice.

76. **por la tarde**   in the afternoon   **Todos los viernes por la tarde cantamos en nuestro Club Español.**
Every Friday afternoon we sing in our Spanish Club.

_____

_____

77. **por ejemplo**   for example   **Hacemos muchas cosas juntos; por ejemplo, comemos en un restaurante español.**
We do many things together; for example, we eat in a Spanish restaurant.

_____

_____

78. **algunas veces**   sometimes   **Algunas veces bailamos.**
Sometimes we dance.

_____

_____

79. **al centro**   downtown   **Vamos al centro de vez en cuando.**
We go downtown from time to time.

_____

_____

80. **a menudo**   often   **A menudo vamos al cine a ver películas españolas.**
We often go to the movies to see Spanish films.

_____

_____

II. On the line write in Spanish one word that will make the sentence meaningful and grammatically correct.

1. **Todos los viernes por la** _____ **cantamos en nuestro Club Español.**

2. **Hacemos muchas cosas juntos; por** _____, **comemos en un restaurante español.**

3. **Algunas** _____ **bailamos.**

4. **Vamos al** _____ **de vez en cuando.**

5. **A menudo vamos al cine** _____ **ver películas españolas.**

III.   **Lists.** In the spaces below, write a list of words in Spanish as directed in each situation.

    A. Look at this picture of the man eating. Write words you would use when telling someone about this scene.

El apetito se abre al comer.
Appetite comes while eating.

1. _____ 3. _____ 5. _____

2. _____ 4. _____ 6. _____

    B. You are a member of a Spanish Club. Write words and expressions you would use when telling someone what the members do in the club.

1. _____ 2. _____ 3. _____

IV.   Answer the following questions in Spanish. You may write a complete sentence or only two or three words. Your answers must show that you understood the questions. What you write must be comprehensible. Just **sí** or **no** is not acceptable.

1. **¿Es Ud. socio del Club Español?** _____

_____

2. **¿Cuántos socios hay en el Club?** _____

_____

3. **¿Qué hacen Uds. para pasar un buen rato en el Club?** _____

_____

4. **Escriba dos refranes en español y tradúzcalos al inglés.** _____

_____

Write the heading in Spanish.

_____

_____

Tengo dolor de cabeza.

(I have a headache.)

I.   Write two sentences of your own in Spanish using the expression given. If you are not ready to do that, just copy each model sentence twice for practice.

81. **¿Qué tienes, Miguel?**   What's the matter, Michael?   **¿Qué tienes, Miguel?**
What's the matter, Michael?

_____

_____

82. **tener buena cara**   to look well   **No tienes buena cara.**
You don't look well.

_____

_____

83. **tener dolor de cabeza**   to have a headache   **Tengo dolor de cabeza.**
I have a headache.

_____

_____

84. **Lo siento.**   I'm sorry.   **Lo siento mucho.**
I'm very sorry.

_____

_____

85. **esta noche**   tonight, this evening   **Esta noche voy a acostarme temprano.**
Tonight I'm going to bed early.

_____

_____

II.   On the line write in Spanish one word that will make the sentence meaningful and grammatically correct.

1. **¿Qué tienes, _____?**

2. **No _____ buena cara.**

3. **Tengo _____ de cabeza.**

4. **Lo _____ mucho.**

5. **Esta _____ voy a acostarme temprano.**

III. Answer the following questions in Spanish. You may write a complete sentence or only two or three words. Your answers must show that you understood the questions. What you write must be comprehensible. Use the vocabularies in the back pages of this book.

1. ¿Qué hace Ud. cuando tiene dolor de cabeza? _____

_____

2. ¿Adónde va Ud. para comprar aspirinas? _____

_____

3. ¿Qué le dice Ud. a su amigo cuando le dice que está enfermo? _____

_____

4. ¿Cuántos años tiene su padre? _____

_____

5. ¿Qué tiempo hace generalmente en el invierno? _____

_____

IV. **Lists.** In the spaces below write a list of words or expressions in Spanish as directed in each situation.

A. Write two expressions in Spanish using the verb **tener.**

1. _____ 2. _____

B. Write Spanish words that are the opposite (antonyms) for each of the following. Use the vocabularies in the back pages and Antonyms in the Appendix.

1. **buena** _____ 3. **día** _____

2. **mucho** _____ 4. **temprano** _____

V. **Writing letters or notes.** Write a note to a friend saying that you are not going to school tomorrow because you are sick and you have a headache. Also say that tonight you are going to bed early. Begin the note with **Querido amigo** or **Querida amiga.** End the note with **Hasta la vista.** Write at least twelve words in Spanish.

_____

_____

_____

_____

_____

_____

_____

_____

_____

_____

Write the heading in Spanish.

_____

_____

Estudio español.

(I'm studying Spanish.)

I.   Write two sentences of your own in Spanish using the expression. If you are not ready to do that, just copy each model sentence twice for practice.

86. **hace dos años que (+ pres. tense)**   for two years (+ pres. perf.)   **Hace dos años que estudio español.** I have been studying Spanish for two years.

_____

_____

87. **hacer lo mejor posible**   to do one's best   **Hago lo mejor posible en la clase de español.** I do my best in Spanish class.

_____

_____

88. **hacer preguntas**   to ask questions   **Hago preguntas en la clase de español.** I ask questions in Spanish class.

_____

_____

89. **enseñar a (+ inf.)**   to teach   **Nuestro profesor nos enseña a escribir.** Our teacher teaches us to write.

_____

_____

90. **seguir (+ gerund)**   to continue (+ pres. part.)   **Pienso seguir estudiando español el año próximo.** I plan to continue studying Spanish next year.

_____

_____

II.   On the line write in Spanish one word that will make the sentence meaningful and grammatically correct.

1. **Hace dos años _____ estudio español.**

2. **Hago lo _____ posible en la clase de español.**

3. **Hago preguntas en la clase de _____.**

4. **Nuestro profesor nos _____ a escribir.**

5. **Pienso seguir _____ español el año próximo.**

Estudio español   **47**

III. Look at this picture of the Spanish teacher and the three kids running out of the classroom. List a few words or expressions in Spanish that you would use when telling about what is going on.

Yo hablo y escribo español.

1. _____ 3. _____ 5. _____

2. _____ 4. _____ 6. _____

IV. Answer the following questions in Spanish. You may write a complete sentence or only two or three words. Your answers must show that you understood the questions. What you write must be comprehensible.

1. **¿Cuántos años hace que usted estudia español?** _____

_____

2. **¿Piensa Ud. seguir estudiando español el año próximo? ¿Por qué?** _____

_____

3. **Mencione Ud. tres cosas que hace en la clase de español.** _____

_____

Write the heading in Spanish.

_____

_____

I.   **Lists.**   In the spaces below, write a list of words in Spanish as directed in each situation.

A. Look at this picture of the man eating. Write words you would use when telling someone about this scene.

El apetito se abre al comer.
Appetite comes while eating.

1. _____   3. _____   5. _____

2. _____   4. _____   6. _____

B. You are a member of a Spanish Club. Write words and expressions you would use when telling someone what the members do in the club.

1. _____   2. _____   3. _____

II.   Answer the following questions in Spanish. You may write a complete sentence or only two or three words. Your answers must show that you understood the questions. What you write must be comprehensible. Just **sí** or **no** is not acceptable.

1. **¿Es Ud. socio del Club Español?** _____

_____

2. ¿Cuántos socios hay en el Club? _____

3. ¿Qué hacen Uds. para pasar un buen rato en el Club? _____

III.   **Lists.**   In the spaces below write a list of words or expressions in Spanish as directed in each situation.

A. Write two expressions in Spanish using the verb **tener.**

1. _____   2. _____

B. Write Spanish words that are the opposite (antonym) for each of the following. Use the vocabularies in the back pages and the Appendix.

1. **buena** _____   3. **día** _____

2. **mucho** _____   4. **temprano** _____

IV.   **Writing letters or notes.**   Write a note to a friend saying that you are not going to school tomorrow because you are sick and you have a headache. Also say that tonight you are going to bed early. Begin the note with **Querido amigo** or **Querida amiga.** End the note with **Hasta la vista.** Write at least twelve words in Spanish.

_____

_____

_____

_____

V.   On the line write in Spanish one word that will make the sentence meaningful and grammatically correct.

1. **Hace dos años _____ estudio español.**

2. **Hago lo _____ posible en la clase de español.**

3. **Hago preguntas en la clase de _____ .**

4. **Nuestro profesor nos _____ a escribir.**

5. **Pienso seguir _____ español el año próximo.**

VI.   Answer the following questions in Spanish. You may write a complete sentence or only two or three words. Your answers must show that you understood the questions. What you write must be comprehensible.

1. **¿Cuántos años hace que usted estudia español?** _____

_____

2. **¿Piensa Ud. seguir estudiando español el año próximo? ¿Por qué?** _____

_____

3. **Mencione Ud. tres cosas que hace en la clase de español.** _____

_____

Refrán   **Quien canta su mal espanta.**   He who sings drives away his grief.

Write the heading in Spanish.

_____

_____

Yo voy al cine.

(I'm going to the movies.)

I. Write two sentences of your own in Spanish using the expression given. If you are not ready to do that, just copy each model sentence twice for practice.

91. **muchas veces**   many times, often   **¿Va Ud. al cine muchas veces?**
Do you go to the movies often?

_____

_____

_____

92. **de ordinario**   usually, ordinarily   **De ordinario voy al cine todos los sábados.**
I usually go to the movies every Saturday.

_____

_____

_____

93. **enfrente de**   opposite   **El cine está situado enfrente de la oficina de correos.**
The movie theater is located opposite the post office.

_____

_____

_____

94. **unas veces**   sometimes   **Mi amigo compra los billetes unas veces.**
My friend buys the tickets sometimes.

_____

_____

_____

95. **a tiempo**   on time   **Siempre llegamos al cine a tiempo.**
We always arrive at the movies on time.

_____

_____

_____

II. On the line write in Spanish one word that will make the sentence meaningful and grammatically correct.

1. ¿Va Ud. al cine _____ veces?

2. De _____ voy al cine todos los sábados.

3. El cine está situado _____ de la oficina de correos.

4. Mi _____ compra los billetes.

5. Siempre llegamos al cine a _____ .

III. In the boxes, print the letters of the Spanish words for the English words next to the numbers. They are in this lesson. They all cross with the Spanish word **cine.**

1. office

2. tickets

3. who

4. always

			C					
			I					
			N					
			E					

IV. Answer the following questions in Spanish in only two or three words, maybe even four. You do not have to write a complete sentence with a subject and verb. Your answers must show that you understood the questions. What you write must be comprehensible. Just **sí** or **no** is not acceptable. If you write a number, spell out the word in Spanish.

1. ¿Va Ud. al cine muchas veces? _____

_____

2. ¿Con quién va Ud. al cine de ordinario? _____

_____

3. ¿Dónde está situado el cine? _____

_____

4. ¿Quién compra los billetes? _____

_____

5. Nombre Ud. cinco frutas. _____

_____

V. **Diálogo.** You just met a friend downtown and you are on your way to the movies. Complete the dialogue using a few words in Spanish.

Roberto: **¿Adónde vas?**

Tú: _____
(Tell him you're going to the movies.)

Roberto: **¿Dónde está el cine?**

Tú: _____
(Tell him it's opposite the post office.)

Roberto: **¿Vas muchas veces al cine?**

Tú: _____
(Tell him you go to the movies every Saturday.)

Write the heading in Spanish.

_____

_____

Pablo no habla a nadie.
(Paul doesn't speak to anyone.)

I. Write two sentences of your own in Spanish using the expression given. If you are not ready to do that, just copy each model sentence twice for practice.

96. **no (+ verb)**
    nadie
    nobody, no one
    Pablo no habla a nadie.
    Paul doesn't speak to anyone. *Or:* Paul speaks to no one.

    _____

    _____

97. **no (+ verb)**
    ninguno (ningún)
    no, not any
    No tiene amigo ninguno. *Or:* **No tiene ningún amigo.**
    He hasn't any friends. *Or:* He has no friends.

    _____

    _____

98. **ya no**
    no longer, not any more
    Ya no viene a nuestra casa.
    He doesn't come to our house any more. *Or:* He no longer comes to our house.

    _____

    _____

99. **no (+ verb) nada**
    nothing, not anything
    No me dice nada.
    He says nothing to me. *Or:* He doesn't say anything to me.

    _____

    _____

100. **no (+ verb)**
     nunca
     never
     No le hablaré nunca.
     I will never speak to him.

     _____

     _____

II. On the line write in Spanish one word that will make the sentence meaningful and grammatically correct.

1. **Pablo no habla a** _____ .

2. **No tiene amigo** _____ .

3. **Ya no viene a** _____ **casa.**

4. **No me dice** _____ .

5. **No le hablaré** _____ .

III. Answer the following questions in Spanish *in the negative*. You do not have to write a complete sentence with a subject or verb. Just one or two words are enough. Answering with just **no** is not acceptable. Your answers must show that you understood the questions. What you write must be comprehensible.

1. **¿A quién hablas en este momento?** _____

2. **¿Tienes hermanos?** _____

3. **¿Qué ves?** _____

4. **¿Hablas inglés en la clase de español?** _____

IV. Print the letters of the Spanish words for the English words.

Verticalmente

2. nothing

Horizontalmente

1. never
3. nobody, no one

V. Write the Spanish word that is an antonym (opposite in meaning). Don't forget to use the vocabulary pages and the Appendix in the back of this book.

1. **algo** _____ 3. **siempre** _____

2. **alguien** _____ 4. **nada** _____

VI. Write five short sentences in Spanish using the negations as indicated.

1. **nadie** _____

2. **ninguno** _____

3. **ya no** _____

4. **nada** _____

5. **nunca** _____

Write the heading in Spanish.

_____

_____

Comenzamos a escribir en español.

(We are beginning to write in Spanish.)

I. Write two sentences of your own in Spanish using the expression given. If you are still not ready to do that, just copy each model sentence twice for practice.

101. **ser hora de**   to be time to   **Es hora de ir a la clase de español.**
    (+ inf.)   It is time to go to Spanish class.

        _____

        _____

102. **prestar atención**   to pay attention   **Hay que prestar atención en la clase de español.**
                                     It is necessary to pay attention in Spanish class.

        _____

        _____

103. **comenzar a**   to begin to   **Este año comenzamos a escribir en español.**
    (+ inf.)   This year we are beginning to write in Spanish.

        _____

        _____

104. **necesitar**   to need   **Necesito papel y lápiz para escribir.**
                            I need paper and pencil in order to write.

        _____

        _____

105. **aprender a**   to learn to   **También aprendemos a leer.**
    (+ inf.)   We also learn to read.

        _____

        _____

II. On the line write in Spanish one word that will make the sentence meaningful and grammatically correct.

1. **Es _____ de ir a la clase de español.**

2. **Hay que _____ atención en la clase de español.**

3. **Este año comenzamos _____ escribir en español.**

4. **Necesito papel y lápiz _____ escribir.**

5. **También aprendemos _____ leer.**

III. Answer the following questions in Spanish. You do not have to write a complete sentence with a subject and verb. Just a few words are enough. Your answers must show that you understood the questions. What you write must be comprehensible. If you use a number, spell it out in a Spanish word.

1. **¿Qué comienzan ustedes a hacer en la clase de español este año?** _____

_____

2. **¿Qué necesita Ud. para escribir?** _____

_____

3. **¿Qué idioma le gusta a Ud.?** _____

_____

4. **Escriba Ud. dos refranes en español y tradúzcalos al inglés.** _____

_____

5. **¿Cuántos años hace que usted estudia español?** _____

_____

IV. **¿Qué hace la señora?**
(What is the woman doing?)

Ella _____

V. After reading the following Spanish advertisement, answer the questions in Spanish using a few words.

> ## PAPELERÍA DE LOS REYES
>
> ☐ papel   ☐ plumas
>   ☐ cuadernos   ☐ lápices
>   ☐ reglas   ☐ gomas de borrar
>
> **282, Avenida de los Reyes, 32011 Madrid**
> **Tel. 34-44-24-72**
>
> **precios reducidos**

1. **¿Cuál es el nombre de esta papelería?** _____

_____

2. **¿Cuál es la dirección?** _____

_____

3. **¿Cuál es el número de teléfono?** _____

_____

4. **¿Cómo son los precios?** _____

_____

5. **¿Qué desea usted comprar en esta papelería?** _____

_____

Write the heading in Spanish.

_____

_____

I.   Write a short paragraph in Spanish consisting of three sentences about going to the movies.

_____

_____

_____

_____

_____

_____

_____

II.   In the boxes, print the letters of the Spanish words for the English words next to the numbers. They all cross with the Spanish word **cine.**

1. office
2. tickets
3. who
4. always

III.   **Diálogo.**   You just met a friend downtown and you are on your way to the movies. Complete the dialogue using a few words in Spanish.

Roberto:	**¿Adónde vas?**
Tú:	_____
	(Tell him you're going to the movies.)
Roberto:	**¿Dónde está el cine?**
Tú:	_____
	(Tell him it's opposite the post office.)
Roberto:	**¿Vas muchas veces al cine?**
Tú:	_____
	(Tell him you go to the movies every Saturday.)

IV. Write five short sentences in Spanish using the negations as indicated.

1. **no** (+ verb) **ninguno (ningún)** _____

2. **no** (+ verb) **nadie** _____

3. **no** (+ verb) **nada** _____

4. **ya no** _____

5. **no** (+ verb) **nunca** _____

V. **¿Qué hace la señora?**

Ella _____

VI. After reading the following Spanish advertisement, answer the questions in Spanish using a few words.

```
┌──────────────────────────────────────────────┐
│            PAPELERÍA DE LOS REYES             │
│                                               │
│  ☐ papel                      ☐ plumas        │
│     ☐ cuadernos               ☐ lápices       │
│        ☐ reglas           ☐ gomas de borrar   │
│                                               │
│  282, Avenida de los Reyes, 32011 Madrid      │
│  Tel. 34-44-24-72                             │
│                                               │
│                          precios reducidos    │
└──────────────────────────────────────────────┘
```

1. **¿Cuál es el nombre de esta papelería?** _____

_____

2. **¿Cuál es la dirección?** _____

_____

3. **¿Cuál es el número de teléfono?** _____

_____

4. **¿Cómo son los precios?** _____

_____

5. **¿Qué desea usted comprar en esta papelería?** _____

_____

Refrán **El tiempo da buen consejo.** Time will tell.

Write the heading in Spanish.

_____

_____

Mi padre acaba de salir de casa.

(My father has just left the house.)

I.   Write two sentences of your own in Spanish using the expression given. If you are still not ready to do that, just copy each model sentence twice for practice.

106. **acabar de (+ inf.)**   to have just   **Mi padre acaba de salir de casa.**
(+ past part.)   My father has just left the house.

_____

_____

107. **hacer una visita**   to pay a visit   **Mi padre va a hacer una visita a mi tío.**
My father is going to visit my uncle.

_____

_____

108. **parecerse a**   to resemble,   **Mi padre se parece mucho a mi tío.**
to look like   My father looks a lot like my uncle.

_____

_____

109. **me gustaría**   I would like   **Me gustaría ir con él a la casa de mi tío.**
(+ inf.)   (+ inf.)   I would like to go with him to my uncle's house.

_____

_____

110. **en lugar de**   instead of   **En lugar de quedarme en casa, me gustaría ir con él.**
Instead of staying home, I would like to go with him.

_____

_____

II.   On the line write in Spanish one word that will make the sentence meaningful and grammatically correct.

1. **Mi padre acaba** _____ **salir de casa.**

2. **Mi padre va** _____ **hacer una visita a mi tío.**

3. **Mi padre** _____ **parece mucho a mi tío.**

4. **Me gustaría** _____ **con él a la casa de mi tío.**

5. **En** _____ **de quedarme en casa, me gustaría ir con él.**

III. Answer the following questions in Spanish. You do not have to write a complete sentence with a subject and verb. Just a few words are enough. Your answers must show that you understood the questions. What you write must be comprehensible. Merely answering **sí** or **no** is not acceptable.

1. **¿Quién acaba de salir de casa?** _____
   _____

2. **¿Adónde va?** _____
   _____

3. **¿A quién se parece mucho su padre?** _____
   _____

4. **¿Le gustaría a usted ir con su padre a la casa de su tío?** _____
   _____

5. **¿Va usted a quedarse en casa?** _____
   _____

IV. **Writing letters or notes.** In Spanish write a note to your cousin telling him or her that (a) your father has just left the house, (b) he is going to visit your uncle, and (c) instead of staying home you would like to go there with him. Start the note with **Querido primo** (if a boy) or **Querida prima** (if a girl). Close the note with **Hasta pronto** (see you soon) and your name. Also, write the date in Spanish.

_____

_____

_____

_____

_____

_____

_____

V. Print the missing letters for the following Spanish verbs used in this lesson.

1. **A ___ A ___ A R**   4. **P ___ R ___ C ___ R**

2. **S ___ L ___ R**   5. **G ___ S ___ A R**

3. **H ___ C ___ R**   6. **Q ___ E ___ A ___**

VI. How many Spanish words can you find hidden in the word **ESTUDIAR**? Find at least four.

> **E S T U D I A R**

1. _____ 2. _____ 3. _____ 4. _____

Write the heading in Spanish.

_____

_____

Yo fui al circo.

(I went to the circus.)

I.   Write two sentences of your own in Spanish using the expression given. If you are still not ready to do that, just copy each model sentence twice for practice.

111. **ayer por la tarde**   yesterday afternoon   **Ayer por la tarde yo fui al circo.**
Yesterday afternoon I went to the circus.

_____

_____

112. **estar de pie**   to be standing   **Un payaso estaba de pie sobre una silla.**
A clown was standing on a chair.

_____

_____

113. **¿de qué color . . .**   what color . . .   **¿De qué color eran sus zapatos? Uno era amarillo y el otro verde.**
What color were his shoes? One was yellow and the other green.

_____

_____

114. **a media voz**   in a whisper   **El payaso hablaba a un mono a media voz.**
The clown was talking to a monkey in a whisper.

_____

_____

115. **reírse a carcajadas**   to laugh heartily, burst out laughing   **Yo me reí a carcajadas.**
I burst out laughing.

_____

_____

II.   On the line write in Spanish one word that will make the sentence meaningful and grammatically correct.

1. **Ayer** _____ **la tarde yo fui al circo.**

2. **Un payaso estaba** _____ **pie sobre una silla.**

3. **¿De qué** _____ **eran sus zapatos? Uno era amarillo y el otro verde.**

4. **El payaso hablaba a un mono a** _____ **voz.**

5. **Yo** _____ **reí a carcajadas.**

III. Answer the following questions in Spanish. You do not have to write a complete sentence with the subject and verb. Just a few words are enough. Your answers must show that you understood the questions. What you write must be comprehensible.

1. **¿Adónde fue Ud. ayer por la tarde?** _____

_____

2. **¿Dónde estaba el payaso?** _____

_____

3. **¿De qué color eran los zapatos del payaso?** _____

_____

4. **¿A quién hablaba el payaso?** _____

_____

5. **¿Cómo hablaba el payaso al mono?** _____

_____

IV. Write a few words in Spanish about something funny you saw yesterday. Tell (a) what you saw, (b) where, and (c) what you did.

(a) _____

(b) _____

(c) _____

V.

¿Qué tiene el muchacho en la mano?

Su respuesta: _____

VI. **Una adivinanza** (a riddle). **Tengo ojos pero no tengo párpados. Vivo en el agua. ¿Quién soy?**

Su respuesta: _____

VII. **Friendly persuasion.** Your friend is making plans to go with you to see the clowns and monkeys at a circus that is in town. You prefer to go to the movies. Write four words or expressions in Spanish that you would use to persuade your friend to go to the movies instead of the circus.

1. _____   3. _____

2. _____   4. _____

Write the heading in Spanish.

¿De quién es esta corbata?

(Whose is this necktie?)

I. Write two sentences of your own in Spanish using the expression given.

116. **¿de quién . . .**   whose . . .   **¿De quién es esta corbata? Es mía.**
Whose is this necktie? It's mine.

_____

_____

117. **fue una ganga**   it was a bargain   **Fue una ganga.**
It was a bargain.

_____

_____

118. **por allá**   over there   **La tienda está situada por allá.**
The shop is located over there.

_____

_____

119. **al otro lado de**   across the street   **La tienda está al otro lado de la calle.**
      la calle   The store is across the street.

_____

_____

120. **de buena gana**   willingly, gladly   **No costó mucho y yo pagué de buena gana.**
It didn't cost much and I paid gladly.

_____

_____

II. On the line write in Spanish one word that will make the sentence meaningful and grammatically correct.

1. **¿De _____ es esta corbata? Es mía.**

2. **Fue _____ ganga.**

3. **La tienda _____ situada por allá.**

4. **La tienda está al otro _____ de la calle.**

5. **No costó mucho y yo pagué de _____ gana.**

III. Answer the questions in Spanish either in complete sentences with a subject and verb or in just a few words.

1. ¿Qué es esto?

_____

2. ¿Dónde la compró Ud.?

_____

3. ¿Dónde está la tienda?

_____

4. ¿Costó mucho?

_____

IV. Write a short paragraph in Spanish containing at least three sentences. Write about something you bought stating its color, where you bought it, where the shop is located, and if you paid a lot or very little for it.

_____

_____

_____

_____

_____

V. **Providing/obtaining information.** You are in a shop because you want to buy a necktie for someone. You are trying to obtain information from the clerk. The clerk is providing you with the information you are asking for. Write in Spanish four words or expressions you and the clerk would use during the conversation.

1. _____   3. _____

2. _____   4. _____

VI. Write four verbs in Spanish used in this lesson.

1. _____   3. _____

2. _____   4. _____

VII. Write four idiomatic expressions in Spanish used in this lesson.

1. _____   3. _____

2. _____   4. _____

VIII. **Lists.** You are going Christmas shopping. Write in Spanish four things that you plan to buy for your friends.

1. _____   3. _____

2. _____   4. _____

IX. Add one letter in any part of the word and get another Spanish word. The word you get is used in this lesson.

1. **gana** (desire) _____ (bargain)

Write the heading in Spanish.

_____

_____

I.   Answer the following questions in Spanish. You do not have to write a complete sentence with a subject and verb. Just a few words are enough. Your answers must show that you understood the questions. What you write must be comprehensible. Merely answering **sí** or **no** is not acceptable.

1. **¿Quién acaba de salir de casa?** _____

_____

2. **¿Adónde va?** _____

_____

3. **¿A quién se parece mucho su padre?** _____

_____

4. **¿Le gustaría a usted ir con su padre a la casa de su tío?** _____

_____

5. **¿Va usted a quedarse en casa?** _____

_____

II. **Writing letters or notes.** In Spanish write a note to your cousin telling him or her that (a) your father has just left the house, (b) he is going to visit your uncle, and (c) instead of staying home you would like to go there with him. Start the note with **Querido primo** (if a boy) or **Querida prima** (if a girl). Close the note with **Hasta pronto** (see you soon) and your name. Also, write the date in Spanish.

_____

_____

_____

_____

_____

_____

III. Write a few words in Spanish about something funny you saw yesterday. Tell (a) what you saw, (b) where, and (c) what you did.

(a) _____

(b) _____

(c) _____

IV.

¿Qué tiene el muchacho en la mano?

Su respuesta: _____

V. **Una adivinanza** (a riddle). **Tengo ojos pero no tengo párpados. Vivo en el agua. ¿Quién soy?**

Su respuesta: _____

_____

VI. **Friendly persuasion.**   Your friend is making plans to go with you to see the clowns and monkeys at a circus that is in town. You prefer to go to the movies. Write four words or expressions in Spanish that you would use to persuade your friend to go to the movies instead of the circus.

1. _____   3. _____

2. _____   4. _____

VII. **Providing/obtaining information.**   You are in a shop because you want to buy a necktie for someone. You are trying to obtain information from the clerk. The clerk is providing you with the information you are asking for. Write in Spanish four words or expressions you and the clerk would use during the conversation.

1. _____   3. _____

2. _____   4. _____

VIII. **Lists.**   You are going Christmas shopping. Write in Spanish four things that you plan to buy for your friends.

1. _____   3. _____

2. _____   4. _____

Refrán   **El ejercicio hace maestro al novicio.**   Practice makes perfect.

Write the heading in Spanish.

La semana pasada
(Last week)

I. Write two sentences of your own in Spanish using the expression given.

121. **la semana
     pasada**   last week   **La semana pasada me caí por la escalera.**
                                 Last week I fell down the stairs.

_____

122. **hacerse daño**   to hurt oneself,   **Me hice daño.**
                        to get hurt   I hurt myself.

_____

_____

123. **romperse**   to break   **Me rompí un dedo.**
                                          I broke my finger.

_____

124. **bajar la escalera**   to go down the   **Me rompí el dedo mientras bajaba la escalera.**
                             stairs   I broke my finger while going down the stairs.

_____

125. **apenas**   hardly, scarcely   **Apenas puedo escribir ahora.**
                                           I can hardly write now.

_____

_____

II. On the line write in Spanish one word that will make the sentence meaningful and grammatically correct.

1. **La semana _____ me caí por la escalera.**

2. **Me hice _____ .**

3. **Me _____ un dedo.**

4. **Me rompí el dedo mientras yo _____ la escalera.**

5. **Apenas puedo _____ ahora.**

III. Write four Spanish verbs used in this lesson.

1. _____   3. _____

2. _____   4. _____

IV. Write four Spanish idiomatic expressions used in this lesson.

1. _____   3. _____

2. _____   4. _____

V. Read the following short paragraph once for general comprehension. Then read it a second time. On the line next to the number, write a Spanish word to complete the thought.

La ____①____ pasada, yo me ____②____ por la escalera. Me hice ____③____ .
Me rompí un ____④____ . Me rompí el dedo mientras bajaba la ____⑤____ . Apenas ____⑥____ escribir ahora.

1. _____   4. _____

2. _____   5. _____

3. _____   6. _____

VI. **Expressing personal feelings.** You are in the hospital because you broke a leg and an arm. A friend comes to visit you. Write four Spanish words or expressions you would use during a conversation about how you feel.

1. _____   3. _____

2. _____   4. _____

VII. Write a note to a friend saying that (a) last week you fell down the stairs, (b) you hurt yourself, (c) you broke a finger, and (d) you can hardly write now. Begin the note with **Querido amigo** (if a boy) or **Querida amiga** (if a girl) and end the note with **Hasta luego** (See you later). Then write your name. Don't forget to write the date in Spanish!

_____

_____

_____

_____

_____

_____

_____

_____

_____

_____

Write the heading in Spanish.

Ayer yo asistí a una boda.

(Yesterday I attended a wedding.)

I. Write two sentences of your own in Spanish using the expression given.

126. **asistir a**   to attend   **Ayer yo asistí a una boda.**
Yesterday I attended a wedding.

_____

_____

127. **llegar tarde**   to be late,   **Llegué tarde.**
to arrive late   I arrived late.

_____

_____

128. **había**   there was,   **Había mucha gente.**
there were   There were many people.

_____

_____

129. **en punto**   sharp (speaking   **La ceremonia terminó a las seis en punto.**
of time)   The ceremony ended at six o'clock sharp.

_____

_____

130. **casarse con alguien**   to marry someone   **Mi amigo Arturo se casó con Elena.**
My friend Arthur married Helen.

_____

_____

II. On the line write in Spanish one word that will make the sentence meaningful and grammatically correct.

1. **Ayer yo asistí _____ una boda.**

2. **Llegué _____ .**

3. **Había _____ gente.**

4. **La ceremonia terminó a las seis _____ punto.**

5. **Mi amigo Arturo se casó _____ Elena.**

III.   **Lists.** You have been invited to a wedding. You are planning to give the bride and groom a present. Write a list of four things in Spanish that you are considering. Perhaps the articles shown below appeal to you. Don't forget to use the vocabulary pages in the back of this book!

1. _____   3. _____

2. _____   4. _____

IV.   You received an invitation to attend a friend's wedding. Write a note in Spanish, consisting of at least twelve words, expressing your acceptance and appreciation. Follow the format of the note you wrote in **Tarea 25.**

_____

_____

_____

_____

_____

_____

_____

_____

_____

V.   **Word Order.** The following words are scrambled. Write them in the correct order to form a sentence that is meaningful and grammatically correct.

1. **boda / a / una / yo / ayer / asistí**

_____

2. **seis / las / a / en / punto / terminó / la / ceremonia**

_____

Write the heading in Spanish.

Tengo miedo de cruzar el parque de noche.

(I'm afraid to cross the park at night.)

I. Write two sentences of your own in Spanish using the expression given.

131. **para (+ inf.)**   in order to (+ inf.)   **Para llegar a mi casa, hay que cruzar el parque.**
In order to get to my house, it is necessary to cross the park.

_____

_____

132. **de noche**   at night   **No me gusta cruzar el parque de noche.**
I don't like to cross the park at night.

_____

_____

133. **tener miedo**   to be afraid   **Tengo miedo de cruzar el parque solo de noche.**
I'm afraid to cross the park alone at night.

_____

_____

134. **tener razón**   to be right   **Usted tiene razón.**
You are right.

_____

_____

135. **por supuesto**   of course   **Por supuesto. Es muy peligroso de noche.**
Of course. It's very dangerous at night.

_____

_____

II. On the line write in Spanish one word that will make the sentence meaningful and grammatically correct.

1. **Para llegar a mi casa, hay** _____ **cruzar el parque.**

2. **No me gusta cruzar el parque** _____ **noche.**

3. **Yo** _____ **miedo de cruzar el parque solo de noche.**

4. **Usted** _____ **razón.**

5. **Por** _____ **. Es muy peligroso de noche.**

III. Look at the picture below. Write four Spanish words or expressions you would use to tell a story about the scene.

1. _____   3. _____

2. _____   4. _____

IV. **Diálogo.** You and a friend are talking on the phone about meeting late at night. Complete the dialogue in Spanish according to the directions.

Elena:	**¡Hola! ¿Qué tal? ¿Cómo estás?**
Tú:	_____
	(Respond by asking how she is. Then ask what she wants.)
Elena:	**Muy bien, gracias. Escucha. ¿Quieres ir al cine esta noche a las diez?**
Tú:	_____
	(Ask her which cinema.)
Elena:	**El cine que está situado enfrente de la oficina de correos.**
Tú:	_____
	(Tell her no. You are afraid to cross the park at night.)
Elena:	**Sí. Tú tienes razón.**
Tú:	_____
	(Tell her it's very dangerous. Suggest next Saturday in the daytime.)
Elena:	**De acuerdo. Está bien. Adiós.**
Tú:	_____
	(Tell her okay, then say good-bye.)

Write the heading in Spanish.

_____

_____

I. Read the following short paragraph once for general comprehension. Then read it a second time. On the line next to the number, write a Spanish word to complete the thought.

La _____①_____ pasada, yo me _____②_____ por la escalera.

Me hice _____③_____. Me rompí un _____④_____. Me rompí el dedo

mientras bajaba la _____⑤_____. Apenas _____⑥_____ escribir ahora.

1. _____   4. _____

2. _____   5. _____

3. _____   6. _____

II. **Expressing personal feelings.** You are in the hospital because you broke a leg and an arm. A friend comes to visit you. Write four Spanish words or expressions you would use during a conversation about how you feel.

1. _____   3. _____

2. _____   4. _____

III. Write a note to a friend saying that (a) last week you fell down the stairs, (b) you hurt yourself, (c) you broke a finger, and (d) you can hardly write now. Begin the note with **Querido amigo** (if a boy) or **Querida amiga** (if a girl) and end the note with **Hasta luego** (See you later). Then write your name. Don't forget to write the date in Spanish!

_____

_____

_____

_____

_____

_____

_____

_____

_____

_____

_____

IV. You received an invitation to attend a friend's wedding. Write a note in Spanish, consisting of at least twelve words, expressing your acceptance and appreciation. Follow the format of the note you wrote in **Tarea 26.**

_____

_____

_____

_____

_____

_____

_____

_____

_____

_____

_____

V. **Diálogo.** You and a friend are talking on the phone about meeting late at night. Complete the dialogue in Spanish according to the directions.

Elena: **¡Hola! ¿Qué tal? ¿Cómo estás?**

_Tú:_ _____
(Respond by asking how she is. Then ask what she wants.)

Elena: **Muy bien, gracias. Escucha. ¿Quieres ir al cine esta noche a las diez?**

_Tú:_ _____
(Ask her which cinema.)

Elena: **El cine que está situado enfrente de la oficina de correos.**

_Tú:_ _____
(Tell her no. You are afraid to cross the park at night.)

Elena: **Sí. Tú tienes razón.**

_Tú:_ _____
(Tell her it's very dangerous. Suggest next Saturday in the daytime.)

Elena: **De acuerdo. Está bien. Adiós.**

_Tú:_ _____
(Tell her okay, then say good-bye.)

Refrán **Si a Roma fueres, haz como vieres.** When in Rome do as the Romans do.

Write the heading in Spanish.

_____

_____

Trabajo de más en más.
(I am working more and more.)

I.   Write two sentences of your own in Spanish using the expression given.

136. **de más en más**   more and more   **Trabajo de más en más.**
                                              I work more and more.

_____

_____

137. **todo el día**   the whole day,   **El sábado trabajé todo el día.**
                          all day   On Saturday I worked all day.

_____

_____

138. **estar cansado(a)**   to be tired   **Cuando llegué a casa, estaba cansado.**
                                               When I arrived home, I was tired.

_____

_____

139. **descansar**   to rest   **El domingo descansé.**
                                     On Sunday I rested.

_____

_____

140. **sentirse bien**   to feel well   **Ahora me siento muy bien.**
                                             Now I feel very well.

_____

_____

II.   On the line write in Spanish one word that will make the sentence meaningful and grammatically correct.

1. **Trabajo de más _____ más.**

2. **El sábado trabajé _____ el día.**

3. **Cuando llegué a casa, yo _____ cansado.**

4. **El domingo _____.**

5. **Ahora me _____ muy bien.**

III. Look at the picture below. Write six Spanish words or expressions you would use to tell a story about the scene. Don't forget to use the vocabulary and Appendix in the back pages of this book.

1. _____ 3. _____ 5. _____

2. _____ 4. _____ 6. _____

IV. Write three sentences in Spanish stating that (a) on Saturday you worked all day, (b) you rested on Sunday, (c) today you are feeling very well.

(a) _____

(b) _____

(c) _____

V. Yesterday was your first day on a new summer job. Write four words or expressions in Spanish that you would use when telling a friend about your work.

1. _____ 3. _____

2. _____ 4. _____

Write the heading in Spanish.

_____

_____

¿Qué pasó?
(What happened?)

I. Write two sentences of your own in Spanish using the expression given.

141. **¿Qué pasó?**   What happened?   ¿Qué pasó?
What happened?

_____

_____

142. **herir**   to injure   **Fui herido en un accidente. No es grave.**
I was injured in an accident. It's not serious.

_____

_____

143. **¡Eso es una lástima!**   That's too bad!   **¡Eso es una lástima! ¿Se siente Ud. bien ahora?**
That's too bad! Are you feeling well now?

_____

_____

144. **todo el mundo**   everybody   **¡Todo el mundo me hace la misma pregunta!**
Everybody asks me the same question!

_____

_____

145. **encontrarse**   to be (health)   **Me encuentro mejor ahora. Gracias.**
I feel better now. Thank you.

_____

_____

II. On the line write in Spanish one word that will make the sentence meaningful and grammatically correct.

1. **¿Qué** _____?

2. **Yo** _____ **herido en un accidente. No es grave.**

3. **¡Eso** _____ **una lástima! ¿Se siente Ud. bien ahora?**

4. **¡Todo** _____ **mundo me hace la misma pregunta!**

5. **Yo** _____ **encuentro mejor ahora. Gracias.**

III. A friend of yours was injured in an auto accident. Write a note in Spanish, consisting of at least thirteen words, expressing your feelings and concern. Follow the format of the note you wrote in **Tarea 26.**

_____

_____

_____

_____

_____

_____

_____

_____

IV. This is a telephone conversation between Señora García and Señora González.

Señora García, on the left, is asking Señora González how she feels. Señora González injured herself in an accident and broke two fingers on her left hand. Write in Spanish the responses according to the directions given in English.

Señora García:	**¡Hola! ¿Matilde? Teresa aquí. ¿Qué tal?**
Señora González:	_____
	(She returns the greeting and says she injured herself.)
Señora García:	**¡Qué! ¿Tu fuiste herida en un accidente? ¿Qué accidente?**
Señora González:	_____
	(She says in a car accident.)
Señora García:	**¡Oh! ¡Qué lástima! ¿Te sientes mejor ahora?**
Señora González:	_____
	(She says everybody is asking her the same question.)
Señora García:	**¿Es grave?**
Señora González:	_____
	(She says it's not serious, she feels better now, and thanks her.)

Write the heading in Spanish.

_____

_____

Fui de compras.
(I went shopping.)

I. Write two sentences of your own in Spanish using the expression given.

146. **pedirle algo a alguien** — to ask someone for something

Le pedí dinero a mi padre.
I asked my father for some money.

_____

_____

147. **al principio** — at first

Al principio, no quiso darme ningún dinero.
At first he didn't want to give me any money.

_____

_____

148. **finalmente** — finally

Finalmente, me dio veinte dólares.
Finally, he gave me twenty dollars.

_____

_____

149. **ir de compras** — to go shopping

Fui de compras. Compré unos libros.
I went shopping. I bought some books.

_____

_____

150. **faltarle algo a alguien** — to lack (need) something

Siempre me falta dinero. Siempre se lo pido a mi padre.
I always need money. I always ask my father for it.

_____

_____

II. On the line write in Spanish one word that will make the sentence meaningful and grammatically correct.

1. **Le pedí dinero** _____ **mi padre.**

2. **Al** _____ **, no quiso darme ningún dinero.**

3. **Finalmente, me dio** _____ **dólares.**

4. **Yo** _____ **de compras. Compré unos libros.**

5. **Siempre me** _____ **dinero. Siempre se lo pido a mi padre.**

III. Write a short paragraph in Spanish containing three sentences. State (a) whom you asked for money, (b) how much he or she gave you, and (c) what you did with the money.

_____ —

_____

_____

_____

IV. Look at the picture. Then, write in Spanish what is asked for in the directions.

A. Write four Spanish words or expressions you would use when telling someone about this scene.

1. _____ 3. _____

2. _____ 4. _____

B. Write four things in Spanish that the girl bought when she went shopping. A new coat that she's wearing? New boots? A pretty dress in her shopping bag?

1. _____ 3. _____

2. _____ 4. _____

V. **Lists.** You are planning to shop for a holiday weekend. Write a list of groceries that you need to buy.

1. _____ 3. _____ 5. _____

2. _____ 4. _____ 6. _____

Write the heading in Spanish.

_____

_____

I. Look at the picture below. Write six Spanish words or expressions you would use to tell a story about the scene. Don't forget to use the vocabulary and Appendix in the back pages of this book.

1. _____ 2. _____ 3. _____

4. _____ 5. _____ 6. _____

II. A friend of yours was injured in an auto accident. Write a note in Spanish, consisting of at least thirteen words, expressing your feelings and concern. Follow the format of the note you wrote in **Tarea 26.**

_____

_____

_____

_____

_____

_____

_____

_____

_____

III. Look at the picture. Then, write in Spanish what is asked for in the directions.

A. Write four Spanish words or expressions you would use when telling someone about this scene.

1. _____ 3. _____

2. _____ 4. _____

B. Write four things in Spanish that the girl bought when she went shopping. A new coat that she's wearing? New boots? A pretty dress in her shopping bag?

1. _____ 3. _____

2. _____ 4. _____

IV. **Lists.** You are planning to shop for a holiday weekend. Write a list of groceries that you need to buy. Use the vocabulary and Appendix in the back pages.

1. _____ 3. _____ 5. _____

2. _____ 4. _____ 6. _____

Refrán **Mientras hay alma hay esperanza.** Where there is life there is hope.

Write the heading in Spanish.

_____

_____

Fui a buscar un regalo.

(I went to look for a gift.)

I. Write two sentences of your own in Spanish using the expression given.

151. **cumplir . . .
     años**

to reach one's . . .
birthday

Ayer mi padre cumplió cincuenta años.
Yesterday was my father's fiftieth birthday.

_____

_____

152. **ir a buscar**

to look for

Fui a buscar un regalo para él.
I went to look for a gift for him.

_____

_____

153. **por todas partes**

everywhere

**Fui por todas partes y al fin compré una
corbata muy hermosa.**
I went everywhere and finally I bought a very
beautiful necktie.

_____

_____

154. **dar las garcias a
     alguien**

to thank someone

Mi padre me dio las gracias.
My father thanked me.

_____

_____

155. **querer a
     alguien**

to love someone

Quiero mucho a mi padre.
I love my father very much.

_____

_____

II. On the line write in Spanish one word that will make the sentence meaningful and grammatically correct.

1. **Ayer mi padre cumplió _____ años.**

2. **Fui _____ buscar un regalo para él.**

3. **Fui por _____ partes y al fin compré una corbata muy hermosa.**

4. **Mi padre me _____ las gracias.**

5. **Quiero mucho _____ mi padre.**

III. Write a story in Spanish, consisting of at least thirteen words, about the situation in the picture below. You may want to say that the cook is a relative, maybe your father or an uncle. Also, you may want to say that he is preparing a meal because it's someone's birthday in your family. Don't forget to use the vocabulary and the Appendix in the back pages.

_____

_____

_____

_____

_____

_____

IV. You have been invited to a birthday party at your friend's house. Write a note in Spanish to your friend, containing at least twelve words, saying that you can't go and give at least one reason. Use the format for writing a note that you used in **Tarea 26.**

_____

_____

_____

_____

_____

_____

Write the complete heading in Spanish.

Una señora salió de una panadería.

(A woman came out of a bakery shop.)

I. Write two sentences of your own in Spanish using the expression given.

156. **salir de**   to come out of, to go   **Una señora salió de una panadería.**
                            out of, to leave   A woman came out of a bakery shop.

                                                       _____

                                                       _____

157. **detenerse**   to stop   **Se detuvo delante de la tienda.**
                                                       She stopped in front of the shop.

                                                       _____

                                                       _____

158. **acercarse a**   to approach   **Otra señora se acercó a ella.**
                                                       Another woman approached her.

                                                       _____

                                                       _____

159. **ponerse a (+ inf.)** to begin (+ inf.)   **Las dos señoras se pusieron a hablar.**
                                                       The two women began to talk.

                                                       _____

                                                       _____

160. **sin duda**   undoubtedly   **Sin duda eran amigas.**
                                                       Undoubtedly they were friends.

                                                       _____

                                                       _____

II. On the line write in Spanish one word that will make the sentence meaningful and grammatically correct.

1. **Una señora** _____ **de una panadería.**

2. **Se detuvo delante** _____ **la tienda.**

3. **Otra señora** _____ **acercó a ella.**

4. **Las dos señoras** _____ **pusieron a hablar.**

5. **Sin duda** _____ **amigas.**

III. Answer the following questions in Spanish. You do not have to write a complete sentence with a subject and verb. Just a few words are enough. Your answers must show that you understood the questions. What you write must be comprehensible.

1. **¿Quién salió de una panadería?** _____

   _____

2. **¿Dónde se detuvo la señora?** _____

   _____

3. **¿Qué hicieron las dos señoras?** _____

   _____

4. **¿Qué se vende en una panadería?** _____

   _____

5. **¿Qué se vende en una pastelería?** _____

   _____

IV. **Lists.** Write Spanish words and expressions according to the directions.

A. Write four Spanish verbs used in this lesson.

   1. _____   3. _____

   2. _____   4. _____

B. Write two Spanish words of things a person can buy in a **panadería.**

   1. _____   2. _____

V. Here are three situations. On the line write a few words in Spanish according to the directions in each one.

A. You are in a bakery in Madrid. The clerk asks you, **"¿Qué desea usted?"** (What would you like?) Tell the clerk what you would like.

   _____

B. You are in a Spanish-speaking country. You are looking for a bakery and you approach a police officer. What would you say to the officer?

   _____

C. You are having dinner in a Spanish restaurant. You would like to have some pastry. What would you say to the waiter or waitress?

   _____

VI. You have been invited to a pot-luck dinner at a friend's house. On the lines write in Spanish two items of food that you plan to bring.

   1. _____   2. _____

Write the complete heading in Spanish.

_____

_____

La chica se puso el nuevo sombrero de su madre.

(The little girl put on her mother's new hat.)

I.   Write two sentences of your own in Spanish using the expression given.

161. **ponerse**   to put on   **La chica se puso el nuevo sombrero de su madre.**
                                     The little girl put on her mother's new hat.

                                     _____

                                     _____

162. **de repente**   suddenly   **De repente su madre entró en el cuarto.**
                                     Suddenly her mother came into the room.

                                     _____

                                     _____

163. **enfadarse**   to get angry   **La madre se enfadó.**
                                     The mother got angry.

                                     _____

                                     _____

164. **en seguida**   immediately   **En seguida la chica empezó a llorar.**
                                     Immediately the little girl began to cry.

                                     _____

                                     _____

165. **al instante**   instantly, at once   **Al instante su madre puso el sombrero en el cajón.**
                                            Her mother put the hat in the box at once.

                                            _____

                                            _____

II.   On the line write in Spanish one word that will make the sentence meaningful and grammatically correct.

1. **La chica** _____ **puso el nuevo sombrero de su madre.**

2. **De** _____ **su madre entró en el cuarto.**

3. **La madre** _____ **enfadó.**

4. **En** _____ **la chica empezó a llorar.**

5. **Al** _____ **su madre puso el sombrero en el cajón.**

III. Answer the following questions in Spanish. You do not have to write a complete sentence with a subject and verb. Just a few words are enough. Your answers must show that you understood the questions. What you write must be comprehensible.

1. **¿Quién se puso el nuevo sombrero de su madre?** _____

_____

2. **¿Quién entró en el cuarto?** _____

_____

3. **¿Por qué se enfadó la madre?** _____

_____

4. **¿Quién empezó a llorar?** _____

_____

5. **¿Qué hizo la madre al instante?** _____

_____

IV. **Lists.** Write Spanish words or expressions according to the directions.

A. Write four Spanish verbs used in this lesson.

1. _____ 3. _____

2. _____ 4. _____

B. Write three Spanish adverbs used in this lesson. One begins with **de,** another begins with **en,** and another begins with **al.**

1. _____ 2. _____ 3. _____

V. Here are three situations. On the line write a few words in Spanish according to the directions in each one.

A. You are in the women's clothing department in a big store in Barcelona. The clerk asks you, **"¿Qué desea usted?"** Tell the clerk what you would like.

_____

B. You are in the men's clothing department in another big store in Barcelona. The clerk asks you what you would like. What would you say?

_____

C. You just bought and paid for an article of clothing in a shop. The clerk was very nice to you. As you leave the shop, what would you say to the clerk?

_____

VI. Change one letter in any part of the word and get another Spanish word. The word you get is used in this lesson.

1. **padre** (father) _____

Write the complete heading in Spanish.

_____

_____

I.   Write a story in Spanish, consisting of at least thirteen words, about the situation in the picture below. You may want to say that the cook is a relative, maybe your father or an uncle. Also, you may want to say that he is preparing a meal because it's someone's birthday in your family. Don't forget to use the vocabulary and the Appendix in the back pages.

_____

_____

_____

_____

_____

_____

_____

_____

II. You have been invited to a birthday party at your friend's house. Write a note in Spanish to your friend, containing at least twelve words, saying that you can't go and give at least one reason. Use the format for writing a note that you used in **Tarea 26.**

_____

_____

_____

_____

_____

_____

_____

_____

III. Here are three situations. On the line write a few words in Spanish according to the directions in each one.

A. You are in a bakery in Madrid. The clerk asks you, **"¿Qué desea usted?"** (What would you like?) Tell the clerk what you would like.

_____

B. You are in a Spanish-speaking country. You are looking for a bakery and you approach a police officer. What would you say to the officer?

_____

C. You are having dinner in a Spanish restaurant. You would like to have some pastry. What would you say to the waiter or waitress?

_____

IV. Here are three more situations. On the line write a few words in Spanish according to the directions in each one.

A. You are in the women's clothing department in a big store in Barcelona. The clerk asks you, **"¿Qué desea usted?"** Tell the clerk what you would like.

_____

B. You are in the men's clothing department in another big store in Barcelona. The clerk asks you what you would like. What would you say?

_____

C. You just bought and paid for an article of clothing in a shop. The clerk was very nice to you. As you leave the shop, what would you say to the clerk?

_____

Refrán **Piedra movediza, el moho no la cobija.** A rolling stone gathers no moss.

Write the complete heading in Spanish.

Fui a la ópera anoche.

(I went to the opera last night.)

I.   Write two sentences of your own in Spanish using the expression given.

| 166. **conocer** | to meet (someone for the first time), to know, to be acquainted with | **Querido amigo: He conocido a mucha gente aquí en Madrid.**
Dear friend: I have met many people here in Madrid. |

| 167. **una vez más** | once more | **Anoche fui a la ópera una vez más.**
Last night I went to the opera once more. |

| 168. **a propósito** | by the way | **A propósito, ¿le gusta a Ud. la ópera?**
By the way, do you like opera? |

| 169. **olvidarse de (+ inf.)** | to forget (+ inf.) | **No se olvide de escribirme.**
Don't forget to write to me. |

| 170. **hasta la vista** | until we meet again | **Hasta la vista.**
Until we meet again. |

II.   On the line write in Spanish one word that will make the sentence meaningful and grammatically correct.

1. **He conocido** _____ **mucha gente aquí en Madrid.**

2. **Anoche fui a la ópera una** _____ **más.**

3. **A propósito, ¿le** _____ **a Ud. la ópera?**

4. **No se olvide** _____ **escribirme.**

5. **Hasta la** _____ .

III. Answer the following questions in Spanish. You do not have to write a complete sentence with a subject and verb. Just a few words are enough. Your answers must show that you understood the questions. What you write must be comprehensible.

1. **¿Dónde conoció Ud. a su mejor amigo(a)?** _____

2. **¿Adónde se va para escuchar buena música?** _____

3. **¿Qué instrumento toca Ud.?** _____

IV. **Lists.** Look at the picture. Then, write in Spanish what is asked for in the directions.

A. Write the names of two places where the actor is performing. At the opera? At the theater? At a concert?

1. _____ 2. _____

B. Write four words you would use when telling someone about this scene.

1. _____ 3. _____

2. _____ 4. _____

V. You are a tourist in Málaga, a beautiful city in southern Spain on the Mediterranean Sea. Write a post card to a friend saying that you have met many people in Málaga and that you went to the opera. Also, ask your friend if he or she likes opera. Tell your friend not to forget to write. Begin the note with **Querido amigo** or **Querida amiga** and end the note with **Adiós.** Then write your name. Don't forget to write the date in Spanish!

Write the complete heading in Spanish.

_____

_____

Pienso en este poema.

(I'm thinking of this poem.)

I. Write two sentences of your own in Spanish using the expression given.

171. **pensar en**   to think of (about)   **¿En qué piensa Ud.? Pienso en este poema.**
What are you thinking of? I'm thinking of this poem.

_____

_____

172. **tener tiempo de (+ inf.)**   to have time to (+ inf.)   **No tengo tiempo de estudiarlo ahora.**
I don't have time to study it now.

_____

_____

173. **dentro de poco**   in a little while   **Lo estudiaré dentro de poco.**
I will study it in a little while.

_____

_____

174. **pensar de**   to think of (about) (showing opinion)   **¿Qué piensa Ud. de este poema? Pienso que es bello.**
What do you think of this poem? I think it's beautiful.

_____

_____

175. **aprender de memoria**   to memorize, to learn by heart   **¡Apréndalo de memoria!**
Memorize it!

_____

_____

II. On the line write in Spanish one word that will make the sentence meaningful and grammatically correct.

1. **¿En qué piensa Ud.? Pienso _____ este poema.**

2. **No tengo _____ de estudiarlo ahora.**

3. **Lo estudiaré dentro _____ poco.**

4. **¿Qué piensa Ud. _____ este poema?**

5. **¡Apréndalo _____ memoria!**

III. Answer the following questions in Spanish. You do not have to write a complete sentence with a subject and verb. Just a few words are enough. Your answers must show that you understood the questions. What you write must be comprehensible. As for the three proverbs you are asked to write in Spanish, they must be complete.

1. **¿En qué piensa Ud.?** _____

_____

2. **¿En quién piensa Ud.?** _____

_____

3. **Escriba tres refranes en español.**

(a) _____

(b) _____

(c) _____

IV. Look at the picture of the man thinking. Then, write three or four words in Spanish to complete the statement.

1. **El señor piensa en** _____

V. Look again at the picture of the man thinking. Then, write four adjectives in Spanish to describe him.

1. _____ 3. _____

2. _____ 4. _____

VI. How many Spanish words can you find hidden in the Spanish word **PENSAR?** Find at least six and write them on the lines.

$$\boxed{\textbf{P E N S A R}}$$

1. _____ 4. _____

2. _____ 5. _____

3. _____ 6. _____

Write the complete heading in Spanish.

_____

_____

Estoy bastante bien, gracias.
(I am feeling quite well, thank you.)

I. Write two sentences of your own in Spanish using the expression given.

176. **¿Qué tal?**   How are things   **Querido amigo: ¿Qué tal?**
Querida amiga: ¿Qué tal?
Dear friend: How are things?

_____

_____

177. **bastante bien**   quite well   **Yo estoy bastante bien.**
I am quite well.

_____

_____

178. **de nuevo**   again   **Estoy en Madrid de nuevo. Llegué la semana pasada.**
I'm in Madrid again. I arrived last week.

_____

_____

179. **echar de menos**   to miss (someone)   **Echo de menos a todos mis amigos.**
I miss all my friends.

_____

_____

180. **prepararse a (para) (+ inf.)**   to get ready (+ inf.)   **Estoy preparándome para volver a mi casa.**
I'm getting ready to return home.

_____

_____

II. On the line write in Spanish one word that will make the sentence meaningful and grammatically correct.

1. **Yo estoy** _____ **bien.**

2. **Estoy en Madrid** _____ **nuevo.**

3. **Llegué la** _____ **pasada.**

4. **Echo de** _____ **a todos mis amigos.**

5. **Estoy preparándome** _____ **volver a mi casa.**

III. You have just arrived in Madrid where you are going to spend one year studying at the **Universidad de Madrid.** You are looking for an apartment. Read the following announcement and answer the questions in three or four words in Spanish.

> **APARTAMENTO BELLO**
> buena vista del parque El Retiro
> 2 dormitorios - 2 baños
> cocina moderna, gran balcón
> cerca del Museo del Prado
> **tel. 34-54-32-69**

1. **¿En qué ciudad está situado el apartamento?** _____

_____

2. **¿Cuántos dormitorios hay en el apartamento?** _____

_____

3. **¿Cuántos baños hay?** _____

_____

4. **¿Es grande o pequeño el apartamento?** _____

_____

5. **¿Cómo se llama el parque cerca del apartamento?** _____

_____

6. **¿Cómo se llama el museo cerca del apartamento?** _____

_____

7. **¿Cuál es el número de teléfono?** _____

_____

IV. You are leaving for Madrid by plane. Here is a copy of your boarding pass. Examine it, then answer the questions.

> **TARJETA DE EMBARQUE**   **NOMBRE DEL PASAJERO** _____
> (Boarding Pass)   (Name of Passenger)
>
> **EQUIPAJE** | **EFECTOS EN TRANSITO**   **3**   **HORA DE EMBARCO** (Time of Boarding)
> (Baggage) | (Items in Transit)
>   13 H. 25
>   (1:25 PM)
> **ESCALAS O DIRECTO**   DIRECTO
> (Stops or Direct)   **FECHA** (Date) 21 JUL
>
>   **NEW YORK A MADRID**
>
> **VUELO** (Flight) 077   **FILA** (Row)   **ASIENTO** (Seat)   **PUERTA DE EMBARQUE**
>   23   F   19
>   (Boarding Gate)

A. Write the Spanish words for the English words.

1. **Boarding Pass** _____   4. **Time of Boarding** _____

2. **Flight** _____   5. **Date** _____

3. **Baggage** _____   6. **Row—Seat** _____

Write the complete heading in Spanish.

_____

_____

I. You are a tourist in Málaga, a beautiful city in southern Spain on the Mediterranean Sea. Write a post card to a friend saying that you have met many people in Málaga and that you went to the opera. Also, ask your friend if he or she likes opera. Tell your friend not to forget to write. Begin the note with **Querido amigo** or **Querida amiga** and end the note with **Adiós.** Then write your name. Don't forget to write the date in Spanish!

II. Answer the following questions in Spanish. You do not have to write a complete sentence with a subject and verb. Just a few words are enough. Your answers must show that you understood the questions. What you write must be comprehensible. As for the three proverbs you are asked to write in Spanish, they must be complete.

1. **¿En qué piensa Ud.?** _____

2. **¿En quién piensa Ud.?** _____

3. **Escriba tres refranes en español.**

   (a) _____

   (b) _____

   (c) _____

III. On the line write in Spanish one word that will make the sentence meaningful and grammatically correct.

1. **Yo estoy** _____ **bien.**

2. **Estoy en Madrid** _____ **nuevo.**

3. **Llegué la** _____ **pasada.**

4. **Echo de** _____ **a todos mis amigos.**

5. **Estoy preparándome** _____ **volver a mi casa.**

IV. You have just arrived in Madrid where you are going to spend one year studying at the **Universidad de Madrid.** You are looking for an apartment. Read the following announcement and answer the questions in three or four words in Spanish.

> **APARTAMENTO BELLO**
> buena vista del parque El Retiro
> 2 dormitorios - 2 baños
> cocina moderna, gran balcón
> cerca del Museo del Prado
> **tel. 34-54-32-69**

1. **¿En qué ciudad está situado el apartamento?** _____

_____

2. **¿Cuántos dormitorios hay en el apartamento?** _____

_____

3. **¿Cuántos baños hay?** _____

_____

4. **¿Es grande o pequeño el apartamento?** _____

_____

5. **¿Cómo se llama el parque cerca del apartamento?** _____

_____

6. **¿Cómo se llama el museo cerca del apartamento?** _____

_____

7. **¿Cuál es el número de teléfono?** _____

_____

Refrán **El que no se aventura no cruza el mar.**   Nothing ventured nothing gained.

Write the complete heading in Spanish.

_____

_____

Me alegro mucho de hacer un viaje.
(I'm very glad about taking a trip.)

I. Write two sentences of your own in Spanish using the expression given.

181. **dentro de ocho días** in a week **Dentro de ocho días iré a Barcelona.**
In a week I will go to Barcelona.

_____

_____

182. **dentro de quince días** in two weeks **Dentro de quince días iré a Valencia.**
In two weeks I will go to Valencia.

_____

_____

183. **irse** to go away **También, este verano me iré al campo.**
Also, I will go to the country this summer.

_____

_____

184. **soñar con** to dream of **A menudo sueño con ir a Francia.**
I often dream of going to France.

_____

_____

185. **alegrarse de** to be glad about **Me alegro mucho de hacer un viaje.**
I'm very glad about taking a trip.

_____

_____

II. On the line write in Spanish one word that will make the sentence meaningful and grammatically correct.

1. **Dentro** _____ **ocho días iré a Barcelona.**

2. **Dentro de quince días** _____ **a Valencia.**

3. **También, este verano me** _____ **al campo.**

4. **A menudo sueño** _____ **ir a Francia.**

5. **Me alegro mucho de** _____ **un viaje.**

III. Look at the picture below. The woman is looking for certain things to pack in her suitcase because she's going on vacation. Tell where she plans to go, how long she will stay there, and what she will do. On the lines under the picture write six Spanish words or expressions that you would use while telling the story.

1. _____   3. _____   5. _____

2. _____   4. _____   6. _____

IV. **Expressing personal feelings.** You are going on vacation this summer with a friend. You prefer to go to a beach but your friend wants to go camping in the mountains. On the lines below, write four Spanish words or expressions you would use to explain why you prefer to go to a beach and not camping in the mountains.

1. _____   3. _____

2. _____   4. _____

V. **Providing/obtaining information.** You are in a store looking at clothes to buy because you are going on vacation. You are telling the salesperson what you are looking for and you are asking for suggestions. On the lines below, write four Spanish words or expressions you would use in this conversation.

1. _____   3. _____

2. _____   4. _____

Write the complete heading in Spanish.

Comí un poco de arroz con pollo.

(I ate a little rice with chicken.)

I. Write two sentences of your own in Spanish using the expression given.

186. **a eso de**   at about   **Anoche, a eso de las once, bajé a beber un vaso de leche en la cocina.**
Last night, at about eleven o'clock, I went down to the kitchen to drink a glass of milk.

_____

_____

187. **un poco de**   a little (of)   **También, comí un poco de arroz con pollo.**
I also ate a little rice with chicken.

_____

_____

188. **subir la escalera**   to go upstairs   **Después de media hora, subí la escalera. Me quedé en mi cuarto.**
After a half hour, I went upstairs. I stayed in my room.

_____

_____

189. **tratar de (+ inf.)**   to try to (+ inf.)   **Traté de leer un cuento.**
I tried to read a story.

_____

_____

190. **llamar a la puerta**   to knock on the door   **Mi hermano llamó a la puerta, entró y hablamos un rato.**
My brother knocked on the door, he came in and we talked a while.

_____

_____

II. On the line write in Spanish one word that will make the sentence meaningful and grammatically correct.

1. **Anoche, a _____ de las once, bajé a beber un vaso de leche en la cocina.**

2. **También, comí un _____ de arroz con pollo.**

3. **Después de _____ hora, subí la escalera.**

4. **Traté _____ leer un cuento.**

5. **Mi hermano _____ a la puerta.**

III. **Word game.** This activity will help you refresh your knowledge of the preterit (past) tense, **el pretérito.** Complete the words in Spanish vertically by printing the missing letters. Follow the English words in the past tense numbered 1 to 11. You can get help to do this word game by reviewing all previous lessons, by consulting the vocabulary, and by referring to the Appendix where you will find 22 basic Spanish verbs fully conjugated in all the tenses.

1	2		3	4	5	6	7	8	9	10	11
E	L		P	R	E	T	E	R	I	T	O

1. I studied.
2. They called.
3. We paid.
4. He repeated.
5. I began.
6. I brought.
7. He elected.
8. I laughed.
9. I invited.
10. I telephoned.
11. They dared.

IV. **Lists.** Write in Spanish words or expressions according to the directions for each.

A. Write six verbs in Spanish in the preterit tense telling what you did yesterday.

1. _____   4. _____

2. _____   5. _____

3. _____   6. _____

B. You spent last weekend at your friend's house. Write three verbs in Spanish in the preterit tense telling what you and your friend did together.

1. _____   2. _____   3. _____

C. Your pen pal from Mexico wants to know what you like to eat and drink. Write a list of four foods and drinks that you like best.

1. _____   3. _____

2. _____   4. _____

Write the complete heading in Spanish.

_____

_____

Mi padre
(My father)

I. Write two sentences of your own in Spanish using the expression given.

191. **llegar a ser**   to become   **Mi padre llegó a ser abogado después de muchos años.**
He became a lawyer after many years.

My father became a lawyer after many years.

_____

_____

192. **dedicarse a**   to devote
oneself to   **Se dedica a su profesión.**
He is devoted to his profession.

_____

_____

193. **hoy día**   nowadays   **Hoy día los abogados ganan mucho dinero.**
Nowadays lawyers earn a lot of money.

_____

_____

194. **por lo general**   generally   **Hoy día los abogados ganan mucho dinero por lo general.**
Nowadays lawyers generally earn a lot of money.

_____

_____

195. **se dice**   it is said, they say   **Se dice que mi padre es un abogado competente.**
They say that my father is a good lawyer.

_____

_____

II. On the blank line write in Spanish one word that will make the sentence meaningful and grammatically correct.

1. **Mi padre llegó a _____ abogado después de muchos años.**

2. **Se dedica _____ su profesión.**

3. **Hoy día los abogados ganan _____ dinero.**

4. **Por _____ general, los abogados ganan mucho dinero.**

5. **Se _____ que mi padre es un abogado competente.**

III. Look at the picture below. The man is late for work. As you can see, he is leaving the house so quickly that he forgot to finish dressing. Tell where he works, what kind of work he does, why he is late for work, what he is holding in both hands, if he is going to his car or take a bus. You may use these or any ideas of your own. On the lines write eight Spanish words or expressions that you would use in telling a brief story about him.

1. _____   5. _____

2. _____   6. _____

3. _____   7. _____

4. _____   8. _____

Write the complete heading in Spanish.

_____

_____

¿Cómo se dice en español *I love you?*

(How do you say in Spanish *I love you?*)

I.   Write two sentences of your own in Spanish using the expression given.

196. **¿Cómo se dice . . .**   How do you say . . .   **¿Cómo se dice en español** *I love you?* How do you say *I love you* in Spanish? **Se dice** *yo te amo.* You say *yo te amo.*

_____

_____

197. **querer decir**   to mean   **¿Qué quiere decir** *en seguida?* What does *en seguida* mean? **Quiere decir** *immediately.* It means *immediately.*

_____

_____

198. **muchas gracias**   thank you very much   **Muchas gracias, señor.** Thank you very much, sir.

_____

_____

199. **de nada**   you're welcome   **De nada, chico.** You're welcome, my boy.

_____

200. **hasta luego**   good-bye   **Hasta luego.** Good-bye.

_____

201. **adiós**   good-bye   **Adiós.** Good-bye.

_____

II.   On the line write in Spanish one word that will make the sentence meaningful and grammatically correct.

1. **¿Cómo se** _____ **en español** *I love you?*

2. **Se** _____ *yo te amo.*

3. **¿Que** _____ **decir** *en seguida?*

4. **Muchas** _____ **, señor.**

5. **De** _____ **, chico. Adiós.**

III. Look at the picture below. Then, on the lines under the picture, write at least twelve words in Spanish telling a story about what is going on in the scene.

_____

_____

_____

_____

_____

_____

_____

_____

_____

_____

_____

Write the complete heading in Spanish.

_____

_____

I. Look at the picture below. The woman is looking for certain things to pack in her suitcase because she's going on vacation. Tell where she plans to go, how long she will stay there, and what she will do. On the lines under the picture write six Spanish words or expressions that you would use while telling the story.

1. _____   4. _____

2. _____   5. _____

3. _____   6. _____

II. **Expressing personal feelings.** You are going on vacation this summer with a friend. You prefer to go to a beach but your friend wants to go camping in the mountains. On the lines below, write four Spanish words or expressions you would use to explain why you prefer to go to a beach and not camping in the mountains.

1. _____   3. _____

2. _____   4. _____

III.   **Lists.**   Write in Spanish words or expressions according to the directions for each.

A. Write six verbs in Spanish in the preterit tense telling what you did yesterday.

1. _____   4. _____

2. _____   5. _____

3. _____   6. _____

B. You spent last weekend at your friend's house. Write three verbs in Spanish in the preterit tense telling what you and your friend did together.

1. _____   2. _____   3. _____

C. Your pen pal from Mexico wants to know what you like to eat and drink. Write a list of four foods and drinks that you like best.

1. _____   3. _____

2. _____   4. _____

IV.   **Providing/obtaining information.**   You are in a store looking at clothes to buy because you are going on vacation. You are telling the salesperson what you are looking for and you are asking for suggestions. On the lines below, write four words or expressions in Spanish that you would use in this conversation.

1. _____   3. _____

2. _____   4. _____

Refrán   **Cuando el gato va a sus devociones, bailan los ratones.**
When the cat is away, the mice will play.

Appendix

Optional situations for conversational and
   writing skills as enrichment **111**

Antonyms and Synonyms **112**

Review of basic Spanish idioms with dar & darse,
   estar, hacer & hacerse, ser, tener **119**

Twenty-two Spanish verbs fully conjugated in all the
   tenses that you need to use in this book **121**

Verbs used in this book **144**

Numbers **145**

Index of idioms, verbal expressions, proverbs,
   and key words showing their location in this book **147**

Abbreviations **149**

Vocabulary: Spanish and English words in one
   alphabetical listing **150**

Answers to all exercises **161**

Optional situations for conversational and writing skills as enrichment

Directions: You may talk about these situations in Spanish or write about them, or both.

1. **Ask a friend to go see a movie with you.** Tell what the title of the film is, whether it is in English or Spanish, at what time the movie begins, where you can meet and what you plan to do after the movie.

2. **You have just come home very late.** A member of your family asks you where you were and you have to tell the person that you were in a car accident that wasn't serious.

3. **You are in Madrid and you want to spend a few days in the mountains.** You go to a travel agency to get information.

4. **You are going to a birthday party with a friend.** The two of you are in your room figuring out what to wear.

5. **You are taking a walk in Málaga with a friend.** You are both deciding where to go first. You are discussing which tourist area is the best.

6. **You are in a drug store in Barcelona** and you want to buy something for a headache.

7. **You are in a restaurant in Cádiz for lunch** and you can't decide what to order. The waiter or waitress is getting impatient.

8. **You are in a bookstore in Sevilla** looking for a specific type of book about Spain. You find the book, pay for it, and then you ask for the name and address of a good Spanish restaurant that the bookstore clerk can recommend.

9. **You are in a Spanish restaurant for breakfast** and you are trying to decide what to order. Each time the waiter or waitress makes a suggestion, you say you don't like it and you give your reason why.

10. **You go into a pastry shop** and ask the clerk if there are any fresh baked pastries. You ask how much. When you find out how much, you notice that you don't have enough money on you.

11. **You are in an airport in Madrid.** You just missed the plane for New York. Ask a clerk for information regarding the next flight to New York City.

12. **You are in Madrid looking for the Prado Museum.** You approach a policeman for directions but he does not understand English and you speak some Spanish.

13. **You are in a bank in Acapulco** and you want to cash a traveler's check but you don't have any identification with you. Prove to the clerk somehow that you are who you are.

14. **You are having dinner in a cheap restaurant** in a small town in Mexico. You find a fly in the soup. Call the waiter and tell him about it.

15. **You are driving a car with a friend.** You are on a country road in Spain. All of a sudden the car stops. It's about two o'clock in the morning. You and your Spanish friend talk about what to do.

Antonyms

An antonym is a word that has the opposite meaning of another word.

aburrirse, to be bored

divertirse, to have a good time

aceptar, to accept

ofrecer, to offer

acordarse de, to remember (Does **acordarse de** remind you of **recordar,** which means *to remember, to remind*? When you remember something or someone, don't you *record* it in your mind?)

olvidar, olvidarse de, to forget (You might think of the English words *oblivion, oblivious.*)

admitir, to admit

negar, to deny

agradecido, agradecida, thankful (You might think of *grateful* and associate it with **agradecido.**)

ingrato, ingrata, thankless (You might think of *ungrateful* or *ungracious;* there is also the word *ingrate* in English.)

alejarse de, to go away from (In **alejarse de,** do you see the word **lejos,** far? See a picture of a person coming close to you (**acercarse a**) and then that person goes away from you (**alejarse de.**)

acercarse a, to approach (In **acercarse a,** do you see the word **cerca,** near, close by?)

amar, to love

odiar, to hate

ancho, ancha, wide

estrecho, estrecha, narrow

antipático, antipática, unpleasant

simpático, simpática, nice (people)

aplicado, aplicada, industrious

flojo, floja, lazy

apresurarse a, to hasten, to hurry (Picture a person who is hurrying because he or she is *pressed* for time.)

tardar en, to delay (Here you have the cognate *tardy.*)

atrevido, atrevida, bold, daring

tímido, tímida, timid, shy

aumentar, to augment, to increase

disminuir, to diminish, to decrease

ausente, absent

presente, present

claro, clara, light

oscuro, oscura, dark

cobarde, cowardly

valiente, valiant, brave

cómico, cómica, comic, funny

trágico, trágica, tragic

costoso, costosa, costly, expensive

barato, barata, cheap, inexpensive

culpable, guilty, culpable

inocente, innocent

dar, to give

recibir, to receive

débil, weak, debilitated

fuerte, strong

delgado, delgada, thin

gordo, gorda, stout, fat

derrota, defeat

victoria, victory

descansar, to rest

cansar, to tire, **cansarse,** to get tired

descubrir, to uncover (Here is another word with the prefix **des,** which usually makes the word opposite in meaning.)

cubrir, to cover

descuido, carelessness

esmero, meticulousness

desgraciado, desgraciada, unfortunate

afortunado, afortunada, fortunate

destruir, to destroy

crear, to create

desvanecerse, to disappear (Here, you might think of *vanish* to remind you of the meaning of **desvanecerse.**)

aparecer, to appear (For the meaning of **aparecer,** isn't it an obvious cognate?)

distinto, distinta, different

semejante, similar

elogiar, to praise (Here, you might see a picture of a clergyman reading a eulogy in praise of someone.)

este, east

fatigado, fatigada, tired

feo, fea, ugly

gastar, to spend (money) (You might see a picture of a person *wasting* money to remind you of **gastar.**)

gigante, giant

hablador, habladora, talkative

hembra, female

ida, going

ignorar, not to know

interesante, interesting

inútil, useless

juntar, to join

lejano, distant

lentitud, slowness

libertad, liberty

luz, light

llegada, arrival

llenar, to fill

maldecir, to curse (Think of *malediction.*)

menor, younger (Think of *minor.*)

mentira, lie, falsehood

meridional, southern

negar, to deny

orgulloso, proud

oriental, eastern

peligro, danger

perder, to lose

porvenir, future

puesta del sol, sunset

recto, straight

riqueza, wealth

romper, to break (Here, in **romper,** you can see a picture in your mind of something *ruptured* in the sense that it is broken.)

seco, dry

separar, to separate

sucio, dirty

tonto, foolish

tranquilo, tranquil, peaceful

censurar, to criticize (Do I need to suggest to you what word to think of in English for the Spanish **censurar?**)

oeste, west

descansado, descansada, rested (Here, in **descansado,** do you see the Spanish word **cansar** within that word? See the entry **descansar** above.)

bello, bella, beautiful

ahorrar, to save (money) (You might see a picture of a person *hoarding* money.)

enano, dwarf

taciturno, taciturna, silent, taciturn

macho, male

vuelta, return

saber, to know

aburrido, aburrida, boring

útil, useful

separar, to separate

cercano, nearby (Do these two words remind you of **alejarse de** and **acercarse a** given above?)

rapidez, speed

esclavitud, slavery

sombra, shadow

partida, departure

vaciar, to empty (Think of *vacate.*)

bendecir, to bless (Think of *benediction.*)

mayor, older (Think of *major.*)

verdad, truth (Think of *veracity.*)

septentrional, northern

otorgar, to grant

humilde, humble

occidental, western

seguridad, safety

ganar, to win

pasado, past

salida del sol, sunrise

tortuoso, winding

probreza, poverty

componer, to repair (In **componer,** you can see something that is put (**poner**) together in the sense that it is repaired.)

mojado, wet

juntar, to join

limpio, clean

listo, clever

turbulento, restless, turbulent

More Antonyms

You ought to know the following antonyms also.

alegre, happy	**triste,** sad
algo, something	**nada,** nothing
alguien, someone	**nadie,** no one
alguno (algún), some	**ninguno (ningún),** none
amigo, amiga, friend	**enemigo, enemiga,** enemy
antes (de), before	**después (de),** after
antiguo, antigua, ancient, old	**moderno, moderna,** modern
aparecer, to appear	**desaparecer,** to disappear
aprisa, quickly	**despacio,** slowly
aquí, here	**allí,** there
arriba, above, upstairs	**abajo,** below, downstairs
bajo, baja, low, short	**alto, alta,** high, tall
bien, well	**mal,** badly, poorly
blanco, blanca, white	**negro, negra,** black
bueno (buen), buena, good	**malo (mal),** bad
caballero, gentleman	**dama,** lady
caliente, hot	**frío,** cold
caro, cara, expensive	**barato, barata,** cheap
cerca (de), near	**lejos (de),** far
cerrar, to close	**abrir,** to open
cielo, sky	**tierra,** earth, ground
comprar, to buy	**vender,** to sell
común, common	**raro, rara,** rare
con, with	**sin,** without
contra, against	**con,** with
corto, corta, short	**largo, larga,** long
chico, boy	**chica,** girl
dar, to give	**recibir,** to receive
dejar caer, to drop	**recoger,** to pick up
delante de, in front of	**detrás de,** in back of
dentro, inside	**fuera,** outside
despertarse, to wake up	**dormirse,** to fall asleep
dulce, sweet	**amargo,** bitter
duro, dura, hard	**suave, blando, blanda,** soft
empezar, to begin, to start	**terminar, acabar,** to end
encender, to light	**apagar,** to extinguish
encima (de), on top	**debajo (de),** under
entrada, entrance	**salida,** exit
esta noche, tonight, this evening	**anoche,** last night, yesterday evening
este, east	**oeste,** west
estúpido, estúpida, stupid	**inteligente,** intelligent
éxito, success	**fracaso,** failure
fácil, easy	**difícil,** difficult
feliz, happy	**triste,** sad
feo, fea, ugly	**hermoso, hermosa,** beautiful
fin, end	**principio,** beginning
flaco, flaca, thin	**gordo, gorda,** fat
grande (gran), large, big	**pequeño, pequeña,** small, little
guerra, war	**paz,** peace
hablar, to talk, to speak	**callarse,** to keep silent
hombre, man	**mujer,** woman

ida, departure	**vuelta,** return (**ida y vuelta,** round trip)
ir, to go	**venir,** to come
joven, young	**viejo, vieja,** old
jugar, to play	**trabajar,** to work
juventud, youth	**vejez,** old age
levantarse, to get up	**sentarse,** to sit down
limpio, limpia, clean	**sucio, sucia,** dirty
lleno, llena, full	**vacío, vacía,** empty
llorar, to cry, to weep	**reír,** to laugh
madre, mother	**padre,** father
mañana, tomorrow	**ayer,** yesterday
marido, husband	**esposa,** wife
más, more	**menos,** less
mejor, better	**peor,** worse
menor, younger	**mayor,** older
mentir, to lie	**decir la verdad,** to tell the truth
meter, to put in	**sacar,** to take out
mismo, misma, same	**diferente,** different
morir, to die	**vivir,** to live
muchacho, boy	**muchacha,** girl
mucho, mucha, much	**poco, poca,** little
nacer, to be born	**morir,** to die
natural, natural	**innatural,** unnatural
necesario, necessary	**innecesario,** unnecessary
noche, night	**día,** day
obeso, obesa, obese, fat	**delgado, delgada,** thin
obscuro, obscura, dark	**claro, clara,** light
odio, hate, hatred	**amor,** love
perder, to lose	**hallar,** to find
perezoso, perezosa, lazy	**diligente,** diligent
permitir, to permit	**prohibir,** to prohibit
pesado, pesada, heavy	**ligero, ligera,** light
ponerse, to put on (clothing)	**quitarse,** to take off (clothing)
posible, possible	**imposible,** impossible
pregunta, question	**respuesta, contestación,** answer
preguntar, to ask	**contestar,** to answer
presente, present	**ausente,** absent
prestar, to lend	**pedir prestado,** to borrow
primero (primer), primera, first	**último, última,** last
princesa, princess	**príncipe,** prince
quedarse, to remain	**irse,** to leave, to go away
quizá(s), maybe, perhaps	**seguro, cierto,** sure, certain
rey, king	**reina,** queen
rico, rica, rich	**pobre,** poor
rubio, rubia, blond	**moreno, morena,** brunette
ruido, noise	**silencio,** silence
sabio, sabia, wise	**tonto, tonta,** foolish
salir (de), to leave (from)	**entrar (en),** to enter (in, into)
sí, yes	**no,** no
siempre, always	**nunca,** never
sobrino, nephew	**sobrina,** niece
subir, to go up	**bajar,** to go down
sur, south	**norte,** north
temprano, early	**tarde,** late

tío, uncle	**tía,** aunt
tomar, to take	**dar,** to give
unir, to unite	**desunir,** to disunite
usual, usual	**extraño, raro,** unusual
verano, summer	**invierno,** winter
vida, life	**muerte,** death
virtud, virtue	**vicio,** vice
y, and, plus	**menos,** minus, less
zorro, fox	**zorra,** vixen, she-fox

Synonyms

A synonym is a word that has the same or similar meaning as another word.

acercarse (a), aproximarse (a)	to approach, to come near
acordarse (de), recordar	to remember
alabar, elogiar	to praise, to glorify, to eulogize
alimento, comida	food, nourishment
alumno (alumna), estudiante	pupil, student
andar, caminar	to walk
anillo, sortija	ring (finger)
antiguo (antigua), viejo (vieja)	ancient, old
así que, luego que, tan pronto como	as soon as
asustar, espantar	to frighten, to terrify, to scare
atreverse (a), osar	to dare, to venture
aún, todavía	still, yet, even
ayuda, socorro, auxilio	aid, succor, help, assistance
barco, buque, vapor	boat, ship
bastante, suficiente	enough, sufficient
batalla, combate, lucha	battle, combat, struggle, fight
bonito (bonita), lindo (linda)	pretty
breve, corto (corta)	brief, short
burlarse de, mofarse de	to make fun of, to mock
camarero, mozo	waiter
campesino, rústico, labrador	farmer, peasant
cara, rostro, semblante	face
cariño, amor	affection, love
cocinar, cocer, guisar	to cook
comenzar, empezar, principiar	to begin, to start, to commence
comprender, entender	to understand, to comprehend
conquistar, vencer	to conquer, to vanquish
contento (contenta), feliz, alegre	content, happy, glad
contestar, responder	to answer, to reply
continuar, seguir	to continue
cruzar, atravesar	to cross
cuarto, habitación	room
cura, sacerdote	priest
chiste, chanza, broma	jest, joke, fun

dar un paseo, pasearse	to take a walk, to go for a walk
dar voces, gritar	to shout, to cry out
de manera que, de modo que	so that
dejar de + inf., cesar de + inf.	to cease + pres. part., to stop + pres. part.
delgado, esbelto, flaco	thin, slender, slim, svelte
desafortunado, desgraciado	unfortunate
desaparecer, desvanecerse	to disappear, to vanish
desear, querer	to desire, to want, to wish
desprecio, desdén	scorn, disdain, contempt
diablo, demonio	devil, demon
diferente, distinto (distinta)	different, distinct
diligente, trabajador (trabajadora), aplicado (aplicada)	diligent, hardworking, industrious
diversión, pasatiempo	diversion, pastime
dueño (dueña), propietario (propietaria), amo (ama)	owner, master, boss
echar, lanzar, tirar, arrojar	to throw, to lance, to hurl
elevar, levantar, alzar	to elevate, to raise, to lift
empleado (empleada), dependiente	employee, clerk
enojarse, enfadarse	to become angry, to become annoyed
enviar, mandar	to send
error, falta	error, mistake, fault
escoger, elegir	to choose, to select, to elect
esperar, aguardar	to wait for
esposa, mujer	wife, spouse
estrecho (estrecha), angosto (angosta)	narrow
famoso (famosa), célebre, ilustre	famous, celebrated, renowned, illustrious
fatigado (fatigada), cansado (cansada), rendido (rendida)	tired, exhausted, worn out
fiebre, calentura	fever
grave, serio (seria)	serious, grave
habilidad, destreza	ability, skill, dexterity
hablador (habladora), locuaz	talkative, loquacious
halagar, lisonjear, adular	to flatter
hallar, encontrar	to find
hermoso (hermosa), bello (bella)	beautiful, handsome
igual, semejante	equal, alike, similar
invitar, convidar	to invite
irse, marcharse	to leave, to go away
joya, alhaja	jewel, gem
lanzar, tirar, echar	to throw, to lance, to hurl
lengua, idioma	language, idiom
lentamente, despacio	slowly
luchar, combatir, pelear, pugnar	to fight, to battle, to combat, to struggle
lugar, sitio	place, site
llevar, conducir	to take, to lead
maestro (maestra), profesor (profesora)	teacher, professor
marido, esposo	husband, spouse
mendigo (mendiga), pordiosero (pordiosera), limosnero (limosnera)	beggar
miedo, temor	fear, dread
morir, fallecer, fenecer	to die, to expire
mostrar, enseñar	to show
nobleza, hidalguez, hidalguía	nobility

nunca, jamás	never
obtener, conseguir	to obtain, to get
ocurrir, suceder, acontecer, acaecer	to occur, to happen, to come about, to come to pass
odiar, aborrecer	to hate, to abhor
onda, ola	wave
país, nación	country, nation
pájaro, ave	bird
pararse, detenerse	to stop (oneself)
parecido, semejante	like, similar
pasar un buen rato, divertirse	to have a good time
pena, dolor	pain, grief
perezoso (perezosa), flojo (floja)	lazy
periódico, diario	newspaper
permiso, licencia	permission, leave
permitir, dejar	to permit, to allow, to let
poner, colocar	to put, to place
porfiado (porfiada), terco (terca), testarudo (testaruda)	obstinate, stubborn
posponer, diferir, aplazar	to postpone, to defer, to put off, to delay
premio, galardón	prize, reward
quedarse, permanecer	to remain, to stay
rapidez, prisa, velocidad	rapidity, haste, speed, velocity
regresar, volver	to return (to a place)
rezar, orar	to pray
rogar, suplicar	to beg, to implore, to entreat
romper, quebrar	to break
sin embargo, no obstante	nevertheless, however
solamente, sólo	only
sorprender, asombrar	to surprise, to astonish
suceso, acontecimiento	happening, event
sufrir, padecer	to suffer, to endure
susto, espanto	fright, scare, dread
tal vez, acaso, quizá, quizás	maybe, perhaps
terminar, acabar, concluir	to terminate, to finish, to end
tonto (tonta), necio (necia)	foolish, stupid, idiotic
trabajo, tarea, obra	work, task
tratar de, intentar	to try to, to attempt
ya que, puesto que	since, inasmuch as

Review of
Basic Spanish Idioms with
dar & darse, estar, hacer & hacerse, ser, tener

◆

with dar and darse

dar a, to face (**El comedor da al jardín,** The dining room faces the garden.)

dar con algo, to find something, to come upon something (**Esta mañana di con dinero en la calle,** This morning I found money in the street.)

dar con alguien, to meet someone, to run into someone, to come across someone, to find someone (**Anoche, di con mi amiga Elena en el cine,** Last night I met my friend Helen at the movies.)

dar contra, to hit against

dar cuerda al reloj, to wind a watch

dar de beber a, to give something to drink to

dar de comer a, to feed, to give something to eat to (**Me gusta dar de comer a los pájaros en el parque,** I like to feed the birds in the park.)

dar en, to hit against, to strike against

dar en el blanco, to hit the target, to hit it right

dar gritos, to shout

dar la bienvenida, to welcome

dar la hora, to strike the hour

dar la mano a alguien, to shake hands with someone

dar las buenas noches a alguien, to say good evening (good night) to someone

dar las gracias a alguien, to thank someone

dar los buenos días a alguien, to say good morning (hello) to someone

dar por + past part., to consider (**Lo doy por perdido** / I consider it lost.)

dar recuerdos a, to give one's regards (best wishes) to

dar un abrazo, to embrace

dar un paseo, to take a walk

dar un paseo a caballo, to go horseback riding

dar un paseo en automóvil (en coche), to go for a drive

dar un paseo en bicicleta, to ride a bicycle

dar una vuelta, to go for a short walk, to go for a stroll

dar unas palmadas, to clap one's hands

dar voces, to shout

darse cuenta de, to realize, to be aware of, to take into account

darse la mano, to shake hands with each other

darse por + past part., to consider oneself (**Me doy por insultado,** I consider myself insulted.)

darse prisa, to hurry

with estar

está bien, all right, okay

estar a punto de + inf., to be about + inf. (**Estoy a punto de salir,** I am about to go out.)

estar a sus anchas to be comfortable

estar conforme con, to be in agreement with

estar de acuerdo, to agree

estar de acuerdo con, to be in agreement with

estar de boga, to be in fashion, to be fashionable

estar de buenas, to be in a good mood

estar de pie, to be standing

estar de vuelta, to be back

estar en boga, to be in fashion, to be fashionable

estar para + inf., to be about to (**Estoy para salir,** I am about to go out.)

estar por, to be in favor of

no estar para bromas, not to be in the mood for jokes

with hacer and hacerse

hace poco, a little while ago

hace un año, a year ago

Hace un mes que partió el señor Molina, Mr. Molina left one month ago.

hace una hora, an hour ago

hacer caso de, to pay attention to

hacer daño a algo, to harm something

hacer daño a alguien, to harm someone

hacer de, to act as. (**El señor González siempre hace de jefe,** Mr. González always acts as a boss.)

hacer el baúl, to pack one's trunk

hacer el favor de + inf., please (**Haga Ud. el favor de entrar,** Please come in.)

hacer el papel de, to play the role of

hacer falta, to be wanting, lacking, needed

hacer la maleta, to pack one's suitcase

hacer pedazos, to smash, to break, to tear into pieces

hacer un viaje, to take a trip

hacer una broma, to play a joke

hacer una pregunta, to ask a question

hacer una visita, to pay a visit

hacerle falta, to need (**A Juan le hace falta un lápiz,** John needs a pencil.)

hacerse, to become (**Elena se hizo dentista,** Helen became a dentist.)

hacerse daño, to hurt oneself, to harm oneself

hacerse tarde, to be getting late (**Vámonos; se hace tarde,** Let's leave; it's getting late.)

with ser

Debe de ser . . ., It is probably . . .

Debe ser . . ., It ought to be . . .

Es de lamentar, It's too bad.

Es de mi agrado, It's to my liking.

Es hora de . . ., It is time to . . .

Es lástima or **Es una lástima,** It's a pity; It's too bad.

Es que . . ., The fact is . . .

para ser, in spite of being (**Para ser tan viejo, él es muy ágil,** In spite of being so old, he is very nimble.)

sea lo que sea, whatever it may be

ser aficionado a, to be a fan of (**Soy aficionado al béisbol,** I'm a baseball fan.)

ser amable con, to be kind to (**Mi profesora de español es amable conmigo,** My Spanish teacher is kind to me.)

ser todo oídos, to be all ears (**Te escucho; soy todo oídos,** I'm listening to you; I'm all ears.)

with tener

¿Cuántos años tienes? ¿Cuántos años tiene Ud.? How old are you? **Tengo dieciséis años,** I am sixteen years old.

¿Qué tienes? ¿Qué tiene Ud.? What's the matter? What's the matter with you? **No tengo nada,** There's nothing wrong; There's nothing the matter (with me).

tener algo que hacer, to have something to do

tener calor, to feel (to be) warm (persons)

tener cuidado, to be careful

tener dolor de cabeza, to have a headache

tener dolor de estómago, to have a stomachache

tener éxito, to be successful

tener frío, to feel (to be) cold (persons)

tener ganas de + inf., to feel like + pres. part. (**Tengo ganas de tomar un helado,** I feel like having an ice cream.)

tener gusto en + inf., to be glad + inf. (**Tengo mucho gusto en conocerle,** I am very glad to meet you.)

tener hambre, to feel (to be) hungry

tener la bondad de, please, please be good enough to . . . (**Tenga la bondad de cerrar la puerta,** Please close the door.)

tener la culpa de algo, to take the blame for something, to be to blame for something (**Tengo la culpa de eso,** I am to blame for that.)

tener lugar, to take place (**El accidente tuvo lugar anoche,** The accident took place last night.)

tener miedo de, to be afraid of

tener mucha sed, to feel (to be) very thirsty (persons)

tener mucho calor, to feel (to be) very warm (persons)

tener mucho frío, to feel (to be) very cold (persons)

tener mucho que hacer, to have a lot to do

tener poco que hacer, to have little to do

tener prisa, to be in a hurry

tener que + inf., to have to + inf. (**Tengo que estudiar,** I have to study.)

tener que ver con, to have to do with (**No tengo nada que ver con él,** I have nothing to do with him.)

tener razón, to be right (**Ud. tiene razón,** You are right.); **no tener razón,** to be wrong (**Ud. no tiene razón,** You are wrong.)

tener sed, to feel (to be) thirsty (persons)

tener sueño, to feel (to be) sleepy

tener suerte, to be lucky

tener vergüenza de, to be ashamed of

Twenty-Two Spanish verbs
fully conjugated in all the tenses
that you need to use in this book

◆

Subject Pronouns

The subject pronouns for all verb forms on the following pages have been omitted in order to emphasize the verb forms.

The subject pronouns that have been omitted are, as you know, as follows:

singular	*plural*
1. **yo**	1. **nosotros (nosotras)**
2. **tú**	2. **vosotros (vosotras)**
3. **Ud. (él, ella)**	3. **Uds. (ellos, ellas)**

The verbs on the following pages are arranged alphabetically with the infinitive at the top of each page. Note that three regular verbs are included of the **-ar, -er,** and **-ir** type. They are **hablar, aprender,** and **vivir.**

aprender

to learn

Gerundio **aprendiendo** Part. pas. **aprendido**

The Seven Simple Tenses	
Singular	Plural

1 presente de indicativo

aprendo	aprendemos
aprendes	aprendéis
aprende	aprenden

2 imperfecto de indicativo

aprendía	aprendíamos
aprendías	aprendíais
aprendía	aprendían

3 pretérito

aprendí	aprendimos
aprendiste	aprendisteis
aprendió	aprendieron

4 futuro

aprenderé	aprenderemos
aprenderás	aprenderéis
aprenderá	aprenderán

5 potencial simple

aprendería	aprenderíamos
aprenderías	aprenderíais
aprendería	aprenderían

6 presente de subjuntivo

aprenda	aprendamos
aprendas	aprendáis
aprenda	aprendan

7 imperfecto de subjuntivo

aprendiera	aprendiéramos
aprendieras	aprendierais
aprendiera	aprendieran
OR	
aprendiese	aprendiésemos
aprendieses	aprendieseis
aprendiese	aprendiesen

The Seven Compound Tenses	
Singular	Plural

8 perfecto de indicativo

he aprendido	hemos aprendido
has aprendido	habéis aprendido
ha aprendido	han aprendido

9 pluscuamperfecto de indicativo

había aprendido	habíamos aprendido
habías aprendido	habíais aprendido
había aprendido	habían aprendido

10 pretérito anterior

hube aprendido	hubimos aprendido
hubiste aprendido	hubisteis aprendido
hubo aprendido	hubieron aprendido

11 futuro perfecto

habré aprendido	habremos aprendido
habrás aprendido	habréis aprendido
habrá aprendido	habrán aprendido

12 potencial compuesto

habría aprendido	habríamos aprendido
habrías aprendido	habríais aprendido
habría aprendido	habrían aprendido

13 perfecto de subjuntivo

haya aprendido	hayamos aprendido
hayas aprendido	hayáis aprendido
haya aprendido	hayan aprendido

14 pluscuamperfecto de subjuntivo

hubiera aprendido	hubiéramos aprendido
hubieras aprendido	hubierais aprendido
hubiera aprendido	hubieran aprendido
OR	
hubiese aprendido	hubiésemos aprendido
hubieses aprendido	hubieseis aprendido
hubiese aprendido	hubiesen aprendido

imperativo

—	aprendamos
aprende; no aprendas	aprended; no aprendáis
aprenda	aprendan

Sentences using this verb and words and expressions related to it

Aprendo mucho en la escucia. En la clase de español aprendemos a hablar, a leer, y a escribir en español.

el aprendedor, la aprendedora learner	**aprender a + inf.** to learn + inf.
al aprendizaje apprenticeship	**aprender de memoria** to memorize
el aprendiz, la aprendiza apprentice	**aprender con** to study with

dar

to give

Gerundio **dando**   Part. pas. **dado**

The Seven Simple Tenses	
Singular	Plural

1 presente de indicativo

doy	damos
das	dais
da	dan

2 imperfecto de indicativo

daba	dábamos
dabas	dabais
daba	daban

3 pretérito

di	dimos
diste	disteis
dio	dieron

4 futuro

daré	daremos
darás	daréis
dará	darán

5 potencial simple

daría	daríamos
darías	daríais
daría	darían

6 presente de subjuntivo

de	demos
des	deis
dé	den

7 imperfecto de subjuntivo

diera	diéramos
dieras	dierais
diera	dieran
OR	
diese	diésemos
dieses	dieseis
diese	diesen

The Seven Compound Tenses	
Singular	Plural

8 perfecto de indicativo

he dado	hemos dado
has dado	habéis dado
ha dado	han dado

9 pluscuamperfecto de indicativo

había dado	habíamos dado
habías dado	habíais dado
había dado	habían dado

10 pretérito anterior

hube dado	hubimos dado
hubiste dado	hubisteis dado
hubo dado	hubieron dado

11 futuro perfecto

habré dado	habremos dado
habrás dado	habréis dado
habrá dado	habrán dado

12 potencial compuesto

habría dado	habríamos dado
habrías dado	habríais dado
habría dado	habrían dado

13 perfecto de subjuntivo

haya dado	hayamos dado
hayas dado	hayáis dado
haya dado	hayan dado

14 pluscuamperfecto de subjuntivo

hubiera dado	hubiéramos dado
hubieras dado	hubierais dado
hubiera dado	hubieran dado
OR	
hubiese dado	hubiésemos dado
hubieses dado	hubieseis dado
hubiese dado	hubiesen dado

imperativo

—	demos
da; no des	dad; no deis
dé	den

Common idiomatic expressions using this verb

A Dios rogando y con el mazo dando. Put your faith in God and keep your powder dry.
El tiempo da buen consejo. Time will tell.
dar la mano (las manos) a alguien to shake hands with someone
dar de comer to feed
darse to give oneself up, to give in

decir

to say, to tell

Gerundio **diciendo**   Part. pas. **dicho**

The Seven Simple Tenses	
Singular	Plural

The Seven Compound Tenses	
Singular	Plural

1 presente de indicativo

digo	decimos
dices	decís
dice	dicen

8 perfecto de indicativo

he dicho	hemos dicho
has dicho	habéis dicho
ha dicho	han dicho

2 imperfecto de indicativo

decía	decíamos
decías	decíais
decía	decían

9 pluscuamperfecto de indicativo

había dicho	habíamos dicho
habías dicho	habíais dicho
había dicho	habían dicho

3 pretérito

dije	dijimos
dijiste	dijisteis
dijo	dijeron

10 pretérito anterior

hube dicho	hubimos dicho
hubiste dicho	hubisteis dicho
hubo dicho	hubieron dicho

4 futuro

diré	diremos
dirás	diréis
dirá	dirán

11 futuro perfecto

habré dicho	habremos dicho
habrás dicho	habréis dicho
habrá dicho	habrán dicho

5 potencial simple

diría	diríamos
dirías	diríais
diría	dirían

12 potencial compuesto

habría dicho	habríamos dicho
habrías dicho	habríais dicho
habría dicho	habrían dicho

6 presente de subjuntivo

diga	digamos
digas	digáis
diga	digan

13 perfecto de subjuntivo

haya dicho	hayamos dicho
hayas dicho	hayáis dicho
haya dicho	hayan dicho

7 imperfecto de subjuntivo

dijera	dijéramos
dijeras	dijerais
dijera	dijeran
OR	
dijese	dijésemos
dijeses	dijeseis
dijese	dijesen

14 pluscuamperfecto de subjuntivo

hubiera dicho	hubiéramos dicho
hubieras dicho	hubierais dicho
hubiera dicho	hubieran dicho
OR	
hubiese dicho	hubiésemos dicho
hubieses dicho	hubieseis dicho
hubiese dicho	hubiesen dicho

imperativo

—	diigamos
di; no digas	decid; no digáis
diga	digan

Sentences using this verb and words related to it

Dicho y hecho.   No sooner said than done.
Dime con quien andas y te diré quien eres.   Tell me who your friends are and I will tell you who
  you are.
querer decir   to mean
un decir   a familiar saying

empezar

to begin, to start

Gerundio **empezando**   Part. pas. **empezado**

The Seven Simple Tenses	
Singular	Plural

The Seven Compound Tenses	
Singular	Plural

1   presente de indicativo

empiezo	empezamos
empiezas	empezáis
empieza	empiezan

8   perfecto de indicativo

he empezado	hemos empezado
has empezado	habéis empezado
ha empezado	han empezado

2   imperfecto de indicativo

empezaba	empezábamos
empezabas	empezabais
empezaba	empezaban

9   pluscuamperfecto de indicativo

había empezado	habíamos empezado
habías empezado	habíais empezado
había empezado	habían empezado

3   pretérito

empecé	empezamos
empezaste	empezasteis
empezó	empezaron

10   pretérito anterior

hube empezado	hubimos empezado
hubiste empezado	hubisteis empezado
hubo empezado	hubieron empezado

4   futuro

empezaré	empezaremos
empezarás	empezaréis
empezará	empezarán

11   futuro perfecto

habré empezado	habremos empezado
habrás empezado	habréis empezado
habrá empezado	habrán empezado

5   potencial simple

empezaría	empezaríamos
empezarías	empezaríais
empezaría	empezarían

12   potencial compuesto

habría empezado	habríamos empezado
habrías empezado	habríais empezado
habría empezado	habrían empezado

6   presente de subjuntivo

empiece	empecemos
empieces	empecéis
empiece	empiecen

13   perfecto de subjuntivo

haya empezado	hayamos empezado
hayas empezado	hayáis empezado
haya empezado	hayan empezado

7   imperfecto de subjuntivo

empezara	empezáramos
empezaras	empezarais
empezara	empezaran
OR	
empezase	empezásemos
empezases	empezaseis
empezase	empezasen

14   pluscuamperfecto de subjuntivo

hubiera empezado	hubiéramos empezado
hubieras empezado	hubierais empezado
hubiera empezado	hubieran empezado
OR	
hubiese empezado	hubiésemos empezado
hubieses empezado	hubieseis empezado
hubiese empezado	hubiesen empezado

imperativo

—	empecemos
empieza; no empieces	empezad; no empecéis
empiece	empiecen

Common idiomatic expressions using this verb

empezar por + inf.   to begin by + pres. part.
empezar a + inf.   to begin + inf.; **Ricardo empieza a escribir en inglés.**
para empezar   to begin with

escribir

to write

Gerundio **escribiendo**   Part. pas. **escrito**

The Seven Simple Tenses	
Singular	Plural

The Seven Compound Tenses	
Singular	Plural

1 presente de indicativo

escribo	escribimos
escribes	escribís
escribe	escriben

8 perfecto de indicativo

he escrito	hemos escrito
has escrito	habéis escrito
ha escrito	han escrito

2 imperfecto de indicativo

escribía	escribíamos
escribías	escribíais
escribía	escribían

9 pluscuamperfecto de indicativo

había escrito	habíamos escrito
habías escrito	habíais escrito
había escrito	habían escrito

3 pretérito

escribí	escribimos
escribiste	escribisteis
escribió	escribieron

10 pretérito anterior

hube escrito	hubimos escrito
hubiste escrito	hubisteis escrito
hubo escrito	hubieron escrito

4 futuro

escribiré	escribiremos
escribirás	escribiréis
escribirá	escribirán

11 futuro perfecto

habré escrito	habremos escrito
habrás escrito	habréis escrito
habrá escrito	habrán escrito

5 potencial simple

escribiría	escribiríamos
escribirías	escribiríais
escribiría	escribirían

12 potencial compuesto

habría escrito	habríamos escrito
habrías escrito	habríais escrito
habría escrito	habrían escrito

6 presente de subjuntivo

escriba	escribamos
escribas	escribáis
escriba	escriban

13 perfecto de subjuntivo

haya escrito	hayamos escrito
hayas escrito	hayáis escrito
haya escrito	hayan escrito

7 imperfecto de subjuntivo

escribiera	escribiéramos
escribieras	escribierais
escribiera	escribieran
OR	
escribiese	escribiésemos
escribieses	escribieseis
escribiese	escribiesen

14 pluscuamperfecto de subjuntivo

hubiera escrito	hubiéramos escrito
hubieras escrito	hubierais escrito
hubiera escrito	hubieran escrito
OR	
hubiese escrito	hubiésemos escrito
hubieses escrito	hubieseis escrito
hubiese escrito	hubiesen escrito

imperativo

—	escribamos
escribe; no escribas	escribid; no escribáis
escriba	escriban

Words and expressions related to this verb

una máquina de escribir typewriter
escribir a máquina to typewrite
un escritorio writing desk
escritor, escritora writer, author
por escrito in writing

escribir a mano to write by hand
describir to describe
la descripción description
descriptor, descriptora describer

estar

to be

Gerundio **estando**   Part. pas. **estado**

The Seven Simple Tenses		The Seven Compound Tenses	
Singular	Plural	Singular	Plural

1 presente de indicativo

estoy	estamos		
estás	estáis		
está	están		

8 perfecto de indicativo

he estado	hemos estado
has estado	habéis estado
ha estado	han estado

2 imperfecto de indicativo

estaba	estábamos
estabas	estabais
estaba	estaban

9 pluscuamperfecto de indicativo

había estado	habíamos estado
habías estado	habíais estado
había estado	habían estado

3 pretérito

estuve	estuvimos
estuviste	estuvisteis
estuvo	estuvieron

10 pretérito anterior

hube estado	hubimos estado
hubiste estado	hubisteis estado
hubo estado	hubieron estado

4 futuro

estaré	estaremos
estarás	estaréis
estará	estarán

11 futuro perfecto

habré estado	habremos estado
habrás estado	habréis estado
habrá estado	habrán estado

5 potencial simple

estaría	estaríamos
estarías	estaríais
estaría	estarían

12 potencial compuesto

habría estado	habríamos estado
habrías estado	habríais estado
habría estado	habrían estado

6 presente de subjuntivo

esté	estemos
estés	estéis
esté	estén

13 perfecto de subjuntivo

haya estado	hayamos estado
hayas estado	hayáis estado
haya estado	hayan estado

7 imperfecto de subjuntivo

estuviera	estuviéramos
estuvieras	estuvierais
estuviera	estuvieran
OR	
estuviese	estuviésemos
estuvieses	estuvieseis
estuviese	estuviesen

14 pluscuamperfecto de subjuntivo

hubiera estado	hubiéramos estado
hubieras estado	hubierais estado
hubiera estado	hubieran estado
OR	
hubiese estado	hubiésemos estado
hubieses estado	hubieseis estado
hubiese estado	hubiesen estado

imperativo

—	estemos
está; no estés	estad; no estéis
esté	estén

Common idiomatic expressions using this verb

—¿**Cómo está Ud.?**
—**Estoy muy bien, gracias. ¿Y usted?**
—**Estoy enfermo hoy.**

estar para + inf.   to be about + inf.
   Estoy para salir.   I am about to go out.
estar por   to be in favor of

estudiar

to study

Gerundio **estudiando**   Part. pas. **estudiado**

The Seven Simple Tenses		The Seven Compound Tenses	
Singular	Plural	Singular	Plural

1 presente de indicativo

estudio	estudiamos		
estudias	estudiáis		
estudia	estudian		

8 perfecto de indicativo

he estudiado	hemos estudiado		
has estudiado	habéis estudiado		
ha estudiado	han estudiado		

2 imperfecto de indicativo

estudiaba	estudiábamos
estudiabas	estudiabais
estudiaba	estudiaban

9 pluscuamperfecto de indicativo

había estudiado	habíamos estudiado
habías estudiado	habíais estudiado
había estudiado	habían estudiado

3 pretérito

estudié	estudiamos
estudiaste	estudiasteis
estudió	estudiaron

10 pretérito anterior

hube estudiado	hubimos estudiado
hubiste estudiado	hubisteis estudiado
hubo estudiado	hubieron estudiado

4 futuro

estudiaré	estudiaremos
estudiarás	estudiaréis
estudiará	estudiarán

11 futuro perfecto

habré estudiado	habremos estudiado
habrás estudiado	habréis estudiado
habrá estudiado	habrán estudiado

5 potencial simple

estudiaría	estudiaríamos
estudiarías	estudiaríais
estudiaría	estudiarían

12 potencial compuesto

habría estudiado	habríamos estudiado
habrías estudiado	habríais estudiado
habría estudiado	habrían estudiado

6 presente de subjuntivo

estudie	estudiemos
estudies	estudiéis
estudie	estudien

13 perfecto de subjuntivo

haya estudiado	hayamos estudiado
hayas estudiado	hayáis estudiado
haya estudiado	hayan estudiado

7 imperfecto de subjuntivo

estudiara	estudiáramos
estudiaras	estudiarais
estudiara	estudiaran
OR	
estudiase	estudiásemos
estudiases	estudiaseis
estudiase	estudiasen

14 pluscuamperfecto de subjuntivo

hubiera estudiado	hubiéramos estudiado
hubieras estudiado	hubierais estudiado
hubiera estudiado	hubieran estudiado
OR	
hubiese estudiado	hubiésemos estudiado
hubieses estudiado	hubieseis estudiado
hubiese estudiado	hubiesen estudiado

imperativo

—	estudiemos
estudia; no estudies	estudiad; no estudiéis
estudie	estudien

Words related to this verb

un, una estudiante   student
el estudio   study, studio, study room
estudioso, estudiosa   studious

altos estudios   advanced studies
estudiosamente   studiously

haber

to have (as an auxiliary, helping verb to form the compound tenses)

Gerundio **habiendo**   Part. pas. **habido**

The Seven Simple Tenses		The Seven Compound Tenses	
Singular	Plural	Singular	Plural

1 presente de indicativo		8 perfecto de indicativo	
he	hemos	he habido	hemos habido
has	habéis	has habido	habéis habido
ha	han	ha habido	han habido

2 imperfecto de indicativo		9 pluscuamperfecto de indicativo	
había	habíamos	había habido	habíamos habido
habías	habíais	habías habido	habíais habido
había	habían	había habido	habían habido

3 pretérito		10 pretérito anterior	
hube	hubimos	hube habido	hubimos habido
hubiste	hubisteis	hubiste habido	hubisteis habido
hubo	hubieron	hubo habido	hubieron habido

4 futuro		11 futuro perfecto	
habré	habremos	habré habido	habremos habido
habrás	habréis	habrás habido	habréis habido
habrá	habrán	habrá habido	habrán habido

5 potencial simple		12 potencial compuesto	
habría	habríamos	habría habido	habríamos habido
habrías	habríais	habrías habido	habríais habido
habría	habrían	habría habido	habrían habido

6 presente de subjuntivo		13 perfecto de subjuntivo	
haya	hayamos	haya habido	hayamos habido
hayas	hayáis	hayas habido	hayáis habido
haya	hayan	haya habido	hayan habido

7 imperfecto de subjuntivo		14 pluscuamperfecto de subjuntivo	
hubiera	hubiéramos	hubiera habido	hubiéramos habido
hubieras	hubierais	hubieras habido	hubierais habido
hubiera	hubieran	hubiera habido	hubieran habido
OR		OR	
hubiese	hubiésemos	hubiese habido	hubiésemos habido
hubieses	hubieseis	hubieses habido	hubieseis habido
hubiese	hubiesen	hubiese habido	hubiesen habido

imperativo	
—	hayamos
he; no hayas	habed; no hayáis
haya	hayan

Words and expressions related to this verb

el haber   credit (in bookkeeping)
los haberes   assets, possessions, property
habérselas con alguien   to have a showdown with someone

hablar

to talk, to speak

Gerundio **hablando**   Part. pas. **hablado**

The Seven Simple Tenses			The Seven Compound Tenses	
Singular	Plural		Singular	Plural
1 presente de indicativo			**8 perfecto de indicativo**	
hablo	hablamos		he hablado	hemos hablado
hablas	habláis		has hablado	habéis hablado
habla	hablan		ha hablado	han hablado
2 imperfecto de indicativo			**9 pluscuamperfecto de indicativo**	
hablaba	hablábamos		había hablado	habíamos hablado
hablabas	hablabais		habías hablado	habíais hablado
hablaba	hablaban		había hablado	habían hablado
3 pretérito			**10 pretérito anterior**	
hablé	hablamos		hube hablado	hubimos hablado
hablaste	hablasteis		hubiste hablado	hubisteis hablado
habló	hablaban		hubo hablado	hubieron hablado
4 futuro			**11 futuro perfecto**	
hablaré	hablaremos		habré hablado	habremos hablado
hablarás	hablaréis		habrás hablado	habréis hablado
hablará	hablarán		habrá hablado	habrán hablado
5 potencial simple			**12 potencial compuesto**	
hablaría	hablaríamos		habría hablado	habríamos hablado
hablarías	hablaríais		habrías hablado	habríais hablado
hablaría	hablarían		habría hablado	habrían hablado
6 presente de subjuntivo			**13 perfecto de subjuntivo**	
hable	hablemos		haya hablado	hayamos hablado
hables	habléis		hayas hablado	hayáis hablado
hable	hablen		haya hablado	hayan hablado
7 imperfecto de subjuntivo			**14 pluscuamperfecto de subjuntivo**	
hablara	habláramos		hubiera hablado	hubiéramos hablado
hablaras	hablarais		hubieras hablado	hubierais hablado
hablara	hablaran		hubiera hablado	hubieran hablado
OR			OR	
hablase	hablásemos		hubiese hablado	hubiésemos hablado
hablases	hablaseis		hubieses hablado	hubieseis hablado
hablase	hablasen		hubiese hablado	hubiesen hablado

imperativo

—	hablemos
habla; no hables	hablad; no habléis
hable	hablen

Words and expressions related to this verb

hablador, habladora   talkative, chatterbox
hablar a gritos   to shout
hablar entre dientes   to mumble
de habla inglesa   English-speaking

la habladuría   gossip, idle rumor
de habla española   Spanish-speaking
hablar al oído   to whisper in one's ear

hacer

to do, to make

Gerundio **haciendo**   Part. pas. **hecho**

The Seven Simple Tenses	
Singular	Plural

1 presente de indicativo

hago	hacemos
haces	hacéis
hace	hacen

2 imperfecto de indicativo

hacía	hacíamos
hacías	hacíais
hacía	hacían

3 pretérito

hice	hicimos
hiciste	hicisteis
hizo	hicieron

4 futuro

haré	haremos
harás	haréis
hará	harán

5 potencial simple

haría	haríamos
harías	haríais
haría	harían

6 presente de subjuntivo

haga	hagamos
hagas	hagáis
haga	hagan

7 imperfecto de subjuntivo

hiciera	hiciéramos
hicieras	hicierais
hiciera	hicieran
OR	
hiciese	hiciésemos
hicieses	hicieseis
hiciese	hiciesen

The Seven Compound Tenses	
Singular	Plural

8 perfecto de indicativo

he hecho	hemos hecho
has hecho	habéis hecho
ha hecho	han hecho

9 pluscuamperfecto de indicativo

había hecho	habíamos hecho
habías hecho	habíais hecho
había hecho	habían hecho

10 pretérito anterior

hube hecho	hubimos hecho
hubiste hecho	hubisteis hecho
hubo hecho	hubieron hecho

11 futuro perfecto

habré hecho	habremos hecho
habrás hecho	habréis hecho
habrá hecho	habrán hecho

12 potencial compuesto

habría hecho	habríamos hecho
habrías hecho	habríais hecho
habría hecho	habrían hecho

13 perfecto de subjuntivo

haya hecho	hayamos hecho
hayas hecho	hayáis hecho
haya hecho	hayan hecho

14 pluscuamperfecto de subjuntivo

hubiera hecho	hubiéramos hecho
hubieras hecho	hubierais hecho
hubiera hecho	hubieran hecho
OR	
hubiese hecho	hubiésemos hecho
hubieses hecho	hubieseis hecho
hubiese hecho	hubiesen hecho

imperativo

—	**hagamos**
haz; no hagas	**haced; no hagáis**
haga	**hagan**

Common idiomatic expressions using this verb

Dicho y hecho.   No sooner said than done.
La práctica hace maestro al novicio.   Practice makes perfect.
Si a Roma fueres, haz como vieres.   When in Rome do as the Romans do.

invitar

to invite

Gerundio **invitando**   Part. pas. **invitado**

The Seven Simple Tenses	
Singular	Plural

The Seven Compound Tenses	
Singular	Plural

1 presente de indicativo

Singular	Plural
invito	invitamos
invitas	invitáis
invita	invitan

8 perfecto de indicativo

Singular	Plural
he invitado	hemos invitado
has invitado	habéis invitado
ha invitado	han invitado

2 imperfecto de indicativo

invitaba	invitábamos
invitabas	invitabais
invitaba	invitaban

9 pluscuamperfecto de indicativo

había invitado	habíamos invitado
habías invitado	habíais invitado
había invitado	habían invitado

3 pretérito

invité	invitamos
invitaste	invitasteis
invitó	invitaron

10 pretérito anterior

hube invitado	hubimos invitado
hubiste invitado	hubisteis invitado
hubo invitado	hubieron invitado

4 futuro

invitaré	invitaremos
invitarás	invitaréis
invitará	invitarán

11 futuro perfecto

habré invitado	habremos invitado
habrás invitado	habréis invitado
habrá invitado	habrán invitado

5 potencial simple

invitaría	invitaríamos
invitarías	invitaríais
invitaría	invitarían

12 potencial compuesto

habría invitado	habríamos invitado
habrías invitado	habríais invitado
habría invitado	habrían invitado

6 presente de subjuntivo

invite	invitemos
invites	invitéis
invite	inviten

13 perfecto de subjuntivo

haya invitado	hayamos invitado
hayas invitado	hayáis invitado
haya invitado	hayan invitado

7 imperfecto de subjuntivo

invitara	invitáramos
invitaras	invitarais
invitara	invitaran
OR	
invitase	invitásemos
invitases	invitaseis
invitase	invitasen

14 pluscuamperfecto de subjuntivo

hubiera invitado	hubiéramos invitado
hubieras invitado	hubierais invitado
hubiera invitado	hubieran invitado
OR	
hubiese invitado	hubiésemos invitado
hubieses invitado	hubieseis invitado
hubiese invitado	hubiesen invitado

imperativo

—	invitemos
invita; no invites	invitad; no invitéis
invite	inviten

Words related to this verb

invitar a + inf. to invite + inf.
la invitación invitation
un invitado, una invitada guest

el invitador host
la invitadora hostess
evitar to avoid

ir

to go

Gerundio **yendo**   Part. pas. **ido**

The Seven Simple Tenses	
Singular	Plural

1 presente de indicativo

voy	vamos
vas	vais
va	van

2 imperfecto de indicativo

iba	íbamos
ibas	ibais
iba	iban

3 pretérito

fui	fuimos
fuiste	fuisteis
fue	fueron

4 futuro

iré	iremos
irás	iréis
irá	irán

5 potencial simple

iría	iríamos
irías	iríais
iría	irían

6 presente de subjuntivo

vaya	vayamos
vayas	vayáis
vaya	vayan

7 imperfecto de subjuntivo

fuera	fuéramos
fueras	fuerais
fuera	fueran
OR	
fuese	fuésemos
fueses	fueseis
fuese	fuesen

The Seven Compound Tenses	
Singular	Plural

8 perfecto de indicativo

he ido	hemos ido
has ido	habéis ido
ha ido	han ido

9 pluscuamperfecto de indicativo

había ido	habíamos ido
habías ido	habíais ido
había ido	habían ido

10 pretérito anterior

hube ido	hubimos ido
hubiste ido	hubisteis ido
hubo ido	hubieron ido

11 futuro perfecto

habré ido	habremos ido
habrás ido	habréis ido
habrá ido	habrán ido

12 potencial compuesto

habría ido	habríamos ido
habrías ido	habríais ido
habría ido	habrían ido

13 perfecto de subjuntivo

haya ido	hayamos ido
hayas ido	hayáis ido
haya ido	hayan ido

14 pluscuamperfecto de subjuntivo

hubiera ido	hubiéramos ido
hubieras ido	hubierais ido
hubiera ido	hubieran ido
OR	
hubiese ido	hubiésemos ido
hubieses ido	hubieseis ido
hubiese ido	hubiesen ido

imperativo

—	vamos (no vayamos)
ve; no vayas	id; no vayáis
vaya	vayan

Common idiomatic expressions using this verb

ir de compras to go shopping
ir de brazo to walk arm in arm
¿Cómo le va? How goes it? How are you?
Cuando el gato va a sus devociones, bailan los ratones. When the cat is away, the mice will play.

ir a caballo to ride horseback
un billete de ida y vuelta return ticket
¡Qué va! Nonsense!

leer

to read

Gerundio **leyendo**   Part. pas. **leído**

The Seven Simple Tenses	
Singular	Plural

1 presente de indicativo	
leo	leemos
lees	leéis
lee	leen

2 imperfecto de indicativo	
leía	leíamos
leías	leíais
leía	leían

3 pretérito	
leí	leímos
leíste	leísteis
leyó	leyeron

4 futuro	
leeré	leeremos
leerás	leeréis
leerá	leerán

5 potencial simple	
leería	leeríamos
leerías	leeríais
leería	leerían

6 presente de subjuntivo	
lea	leamos
leas	leáis
lea	lean

7 imperfecto de subjuntivo	
leyera	leyéramos
leyeras	leyerais
leyera	leyeran
OR	
leyese	leyésemos
leyeses	leyeseis
leyese	leyesen

The Seven Compound Tenses	
Singular	Plural

8 perfecto de indicativo	
he leído	hemos leído
has leído	habéis leído
ha leído	han leído

9 pluscuamperfecto de indicativo	
había leído	habíamos leído
habías leído	habíais leído
había leído	habían leído

10 pretérito anterior	
hube leído	hubimos leído
hubiste leído	hubisteis leído
hubo leído	hubieron leído

11 futuro perfecto	
habré leído	habremos leído
habrás leído	habréis leído
habrá leído	habrán leído

12 potencial compuesto	
habría leído	habríamos leído
habrías leído	habríais leído
habría leído	habrían leído

13 perfecto de subjuntivo	
haya leído	hayamos leído
hayas leído	hayáis leído
haya leído	hayan leído

14 pluscuamperfecto de subjuntivo	
hubiera leído	hubiéramos leído
hubieras leído	hubierais leído
hubiera leído	hubieran leído
OR	
hubiese leído	hubiésemos leído
hubieses leído	hubieseis leído
hubiese leído	hubiesen leído

imperativo

—	leamos
lee; no leas	leed; no leáis
lea	lean

Words and expressions related to this verb

la lectura reading
  Me gusta la lectura. I like reading.
la lección lesson
lector, lectora reader
leer mal to misread

releer to read again, to reread
leer entre líneas to read between the lines
un, una leccionista private tutor
leer para sí to read to oneself

llamarse

to be called, to be named

Gerundio **llamándose**   Part. pas. **llamado**

The Seven Simple Tenses		The Seven Compound Tenses	
Singular	Plural	Singular	Plural

1 presente de indicativo

me llamo	nos llamamos		
te llamas	os llamáis		
se llama	se llaman		

8 perfecto de indicativo

me he llamado	nos hemos llamado
te has llamado	os habéis llamado
se ha llamado	se han llamado

2 imperfecto de indicativo

me llamaba	nos llamábamos
te llamabas	os llamabais
se llamaba	se llamaban

9 pluscuamperfecto de indicativo

me había llamado	nos habíamos llamado
te habías llamado	os habíais llamado
se había llamado	se habían llamado

3 pretérito

me llamé	nos llamamos
te llamaste	os llamasteis
se llamó	se llamaron

10 pretérito anterior

me hube llamado	nos hubimos llamado
te hubiste llamado	os hubisteis llamado
se hubo llamado	se hubieron llamado

4 futuro

me llamaré	nos llamaremos
te llamarás	os llamaréis
se llamará	se llamarán

11 futuro perfecto

me habré llamado	nos habremos llamado
te habrás llamado	os habréis llamado
se habrá llamado	se habrán llamado

5 potencial simple

me llamaría	nos llamaríamos
te llamarías	os llamaríais
se llamaría	se llamarían

12 potencial compuesto

me habría llamado	nos habríamos llamado
te habrías llamado	os habríais llamado
se habría llamado	se habrían llamado

6 presente de subjuntivo

me llame	nos llamemos
te llames	os llaméis
se llame	se llamen

13 perfecto de subjuntivo

me haya llamado	nos hayamos llamado
te hayas llamado	os hayáis llamado
se haya llamado	se hayan llamado

7 imperfecto de subjuntivo

me llamara	nos llamáramos
te llamaras	os llamarais
se llamara	se llamaran
OR	
me llamase	nos llamásemos
te llamases	os llamaseis
se llamase	se llamasen

14 pluscuamperfecto de subjuntivo

me hubiera llamado	nos hubiéramos llamado
te hubieras llamado	os hubierais llamado
se hubiera llamado	se hubieran llamado
OR	
me hubiese llamado	nos hubiésemos llamado
te hubieses llamado	os hubieseis llamado
se hubiese llamado	se hubiesen llamado

imperativo

—	llamémonos; no nos llamenos
llámate; no te llames	llamaos; no os llaméis
llámese; no se llame	llámense; no se llamen

Common idiomatic expressions using this verb

—**¿Cómo se llama usted?**   What is your name? (How do you call yourself?)
—**Me llamo Juan Morales.**   My name is Juan Morales.
—**¿Y cómo se llaman sus hermanos?**   And what are your brother's and sister's names?
—**Se llaman Teresa y Pedro.**   Their names are Teresa and Peter.

pagar

to pay

Gerundio **pagando**   Part. pas. **pagado**

The Seven Simple Tenses	
Singular	Plural

1 presente de indicativo	
pago	pagamos
pagas	pagáis
paga	pagan

2 imperfecto de indicativo	
pagaba	pagábamos
pagabas	pagabais
pagaba	pagaban

3 pretérito	
pagué	pagamos
pagaste	pagasteis
pagó	pagaron

4 futuro	
pagaré	pagaremos
pagarás	pagaréis
pagará	pagarán

5 potencial simple	
pagaría	pagaríamos
pagarías	pagaríais
pagaría	pagarían

6 presente de subjuntivo	
pague	paguemos
pagues	paguéis
pague	paguen

7 imperfecto de subjuntivo	
pagara	pagáramos
pagaras	pagarais
pagara	pagaran
OR	
pagase	pagásemos
pagases	pagaseis
pagase	pagasen

The Seven Compound Tenses	
Singular	Plural

8 perfecto de indicativo	
he pagado	hemos pagado
has pagado	habéis pagado
ha pagado	han pagado

9 pluscuamperfecto de indicativo	
había pagado	habíamos pagado
habías pagado	habíais pagado
había pagado	habían pagado

10 pretérito anterior	
hube pagado	hubimos pagado
hubiste pagado	hubisteis pagado
hubo pagado	hubieron pagado

11 futuro perfecto	
habré pagado	habremos pagado
habrás pagado	habréis pagado
habrá pagado	habrán pagado

12 potencial compuesto	
habría pagado	habríamos pagado
habrías pagado	habríais pagado
habría pagado	habrían pagado

13 perfecto de subjuntivo	
haya pagado	hayamos pagado
hayas pagado	hayáis pagado
haya pagado	hayan pagado

14 pluscuamperfecto de subjuntivo	
hubiera pagado	hubiéramos pagado
hubieras pagado	hubierais pagado
hubiera pagado	hubieran pagado
OR	
hubiese pagado	hubiésemos pagado
hubieses pagado	hubieseis pagado
hubiese pagado	hubiesen pagado

imperativo

—	paguemos
paga; no pagues	pagad; no paguéis
pague	paguen

Words and expressions related to this verb

la paga   payment
pagable   payable
pagador, pagadora   payer
el pagaré   promissory note, I.O.U.

pagar al contado   to pay in cash
pagar contra entrega   C.O.D. (Collect on delivery)
pagar la cuenta   to pay the bill
pagar un ojo de la cara   to pay an arm and a
    leg; to pay through your nose

querer

to want, to wish

Gerundio **queriendo**   Part. pas. **querido**

The Seven Simple Tenses	
Singular	Plural

1   presente de indicativo

quiero	queremos
quieres	queréis
quiere	quieren

2   imperfecto de indicativo

quería	queríamos
querías	queríais
quería	querían

3   pretérito

quise	quisimos
quisiste	quisisteis
quiso	quisieron

4   futuro

querré	querremos
querrás	querréis
querrá	querrán

5   potencial simple

querría	querríamos
querrías	querríais
querría	querrían

6   presente de subjuntivo

quiera	queramos
quieras	queráis
quiera	quieran

7   imperfecto de subjuntivo

quisiera	quisiéramos
quisieras	quisierais
quisiera	quisieran
OR	
quisiese	quisiésemos
quisieses	quisieseis
quisiese	quisiesen

The Seven Compound Tenses	
Singular	Plural

8   perfecto de indicativo

he querido	hemos querido
has querido	habéis querido
ha querido	han querido

9   pluscuamperfecto de indicativo

había querido	habíamos querido
habías querido	habíais querido
había querido	habían querido

10   pretérito anterior

hube querido	hubimos querido
hubiste querido	hubisteis querido
hubo querido	hubieron querido

11   futuro perfecto

habré querido	habremos querido
habrás querido	habréis querido
habrá querido	habrán querido

12   potencial compuesto

habría querido	habríamos querido
habrías querido	habríais querido
habría querido	habrían querido

13   perfecto de subjuntivo

haya querido	hayamos querido
hayas querido	hayáis querido
haya querido	hayan querido

14   pluscuamperfecto de subjuntivo

hubiera querido	hubiéremos querido
hubieras querido	hubierais querido
hubiera querido	hubieran querido
OR	
hubiese querido	hubiésemos querido
hubieses querido	hubieseis querido
hubiese querido	hubiesen querido

imperativo

—	queramos
quiere; no quieras	quered; no queráis
quiera	quieran

Words and expressions related to this verb

querer decir   to mean;   **¿Qué quiere Ud. decir?**   What do you mean?
   ¿Qué quiere decir esto?   What does this mean?
querido, querida   dear
querido amigo, querida amiga   dear friend
querido mío, querida mía   my dear
querer bien a   to love
Querer es poder   Where there's a will there's a way.

reír

to laugh

Gerundio **riendo**   Part. pas. **reído**

The Seven Simple Tenses		The Seven Compound Tenses	
Singular	Plural	Singular	Plural

1 presente de indicativo

río	reímos		
ríes	reís		
ríe	ríen		

8 perfecto de indicativo

he reído	hemos reído
has reído	habéis reído
ha reído	han reído

2 imperfecto de indicativo

reía	reíamos
reías	reíais
reía	reían

9 pluscuamperfecto de indicativo

había reído	habíamos reído
habías reído	habíais reído
había reído	habían reído

3 pretérito

reí	reímos
reíste	reísteis
rió	rieron

10 pretérito anterior

hube reído	hubimos reído
hubiste reído	hubisteis reído
hubo reído	hubieron reído

4 futuro

reiré	reiremos
reirás	reiréis
reirá	reirán

11 futuro perfecto

habré reído	habremos reído
habrás reído	habréis reído
habrá reído	habrán reído

5 potencial simple

reiría	reiríamos
reirías	reiríais
reiría	reirían

12 potencial compuesto

habría reído	habríamos reído
habrías reído	habríais reído
habría reído	habrían reído

6 presente de subjuntivo

ría	riamos
rías	riáis
ría	rían

13 perfecto de subjuntivo

haya reído	hayamos reído
hayas reído	hayáis reído
haya reído	hayan reído

7 imperfecto de subjuntivo

riera	riéramos
rieras	rierais
riera	rieran
OR	
riese	riésemos
rieses	rieseis
riese	riesen

14 pluscuamperfecto de subjuntivo

hubiera reído	hubiéramos reído
hubieras reído	hubierais reído
hubiera reído	hubieran reído
OR	
hubiese reído	hubiésemos reído
hubieses reído	hubieseis reído
hubiese reído	hubiesen reído

imperativo

—	riamos
ríe; no rías	reíd; no riáis
ría	rían

Common idiomatic expressions using this verb

reír a carcajadas   to laugh loudly
reír de   to laugh at, to make fun of
la risa   laugh, laughter

risible   laughable
risueño, risueña   smiling

repetir

to repeat

Gerundio **repitiendo**   Part. pas. **repetido**

The Seven Simple Tenses		The Seven Compound Tenses	
Singular	Plural	Singular	Plural

1 presente de indicativo

repito	repetimos
repites	repetís
repite	repiten

8 perfecto de indicativo

he repetido	hemos repetido
has repetido	habéis repetido
ha repetido	han repetido

2 imperfecto de indicativo

repetía	repetíamos
repetías	repetíais
repetía	repetían

9 pluscuamperfecto de indicativo

había repetido	habíamos repetido
habías repetido	habíais repetido
había repetido	habían repetido

3 pretérito

repetí	repetimos
repetiste	repetisteis
repitió	repitieron

10 pretérito anterior

hube repetido	hubimos repetido
hubiste repetido	hubisteis repetido
hubo repetido	hubieron repetido

4 futuro

repetiré	repetiremos
repetirás	repetiréis
repetirá	repetirán

11 futuro perfecto

habré repetido	habremos repetido
habrás repetido	habréis repetido
habrá repetido	habrán repetido

5 potencial simple

repetiría	repetiríamos
repetirías	repetiríais
repetiría	repetirían

12 potencial compuesto

habría repetido	habríamos repetido
habrías repetido	habríais repetido
habría repetido	habrían repetido

6 presente de subjuntivo

repita	repitamos
repitas	repitáis
repita	repitan

13 perfecto de subjuntivo

haya repetido	hayamos repetido
hayas repetido	hayáis repetido
haya repetido	hayan repetido

7 imperfecto de subjuntivo

repitiera	repitiéramos
repitieras	repitierais
repitiera	repitieran
OR	
repitiese	repitiésemos
repitieses	repitieseis
repitiese	repitiesen

14 pluscuamperfecto de subjuntivo

hubiera repetido	hubiéramos repetido
hubieras repetido	hubierais repetido
hubiera repetido	hubieran repetido
OR	
hubiese repetido	hubiésemos repetido
hubieses repetido	hubieseis repetido
hubiese repetido	hubiesen repetido

imperativo

—	repitamos
repite; no repitas	repetid; no repitáis
repita	repitan

Words related to this verb

la repetición repetition **repitiente (adj.)** repeating
repetidamente repeatedly **repetirse** to repeat to oneself

ser

to be

Gerundio **siendo**   Part. pas. **sido**

The Seven Simple Tenses	
Singular	Plural

The Seven Compound Tenses	
Singular	Plural

1 presente de indicativo

Singular	Plural
soy	somos
eres	sois
es	son

8 perfecto de indicativo

Singular	Plural
he sido	hemos sido
has sido	habéis sido
ha sido	han sido

2 imperfecto de indicativo

era	éramos
eras	erais
era	eran

9 pluscuamperfecto de indicativo

había sido	habíamos sido
habías sido	habíais sido
había sido	habían sido

3 pretérito

fui	fuimos
fuiste	fuisteis
fue	fueron

10 pretérito anterior

hube sido	hubimos sido
hubiste sido	hubisteis sido
hubo sido	hubieron sido

4 futuro

seré	seremos
serás	seréis
será	serán

11 futuro perfecto

habré sido	habremos sido
habrás sido	habréis sido
habrá sido	habrán sido

5 potencial simple

sería	seríamos
serías	seríais
sería	serían

12 potencial compuesto

habría sido	habríamos sido
habrías sido	habríais sido
habría sido	habrían sido

6 presente de subjuntivo

sea	seamos
seas	seáis
sea	sean

13 perfecto de subjuntivo

haya sido	hayamos sido
hayas sido	hayáis sido
haya sido	hayan sido

7 imperfecto de subjuntivo

fuera	fuéramos
fueras	fuerais
fuera	fueran
OR	
fuese	fuésemos
fueses	fueseis
fuese	fuesen

14 pluscuamperfecto de subjuntivo

hubiera sido	hubiéramos sido
hubieras sido	hubierais sido
hubiera sido	hubieran sido
OR	
hubiese sido	hubiésemos sido
hubieses sido	hubieseis sido
hubiese sido	hubiesen sido

imperativo

—	seamos
sé; no seas	sed; no seáis
sea	sean

Common idiomatic expressions using this verb

Dime con quien andas y te diré quien eres. Tell me who your friends are and I will tell you who you are.

es decir that is, that is to say; **Si yo fuera usted. . .** If I were you. . .

¿Qué hora es? What time is it? **Es la una.** It is one o'clock. **Son las dos.** It is two o'clock.

telefonear

to telephone

Gerundio **telefoneando**　　Part. pas. **telefoneado**

The Seven Simple Tenses		The Seven Compound Tenses	
Singular	Plural	Singular	Plural

1　presente de indicativo

		8　perfecto de indicativo	
telefoneo	telefoneamos	he telefoneado	hemos telefoneado
telefoneas	telefoneáis	has telefoneado	habéis telefoneado
telefonea	telefonean	ha telefoneado	han telefoneado

2　imperfecto de indicativo

		9　pluscuamperfecto de indicativo	
telefoneaba	telefoneábamos	había telefoneado	habíamos telefoneado
telefoneabas	telefoneabais	habías telefoneado	habíais telefoneado
telefoneaba	telefoneaban	había telefoneado	habían telefoneado

3　pretérito

		10　pretérito anterior	
telefoneé	telefoneamos	hube telefoneado	hubimos telefoneado
telefoneaste	telefoneasteis	hubiste telefoneado	hubisteis telefoneado
telefoneó	telefonearon	hubo telefoneado	hubieron telefoneado

4　futuro

		11　futuro perfecto	
telefonearé	telefonearemos	habré telefoneado	habremos telefoneado
telefonearás	telefonearéis	habrás telefoneado	habréis telefoneado
telefoneará	telefonearán	habrá telefoneado	habrán telefoneado

5　potencial simple

		12　potencial compuesto	
telefonearía	telefonearíamos	habría telefoneado	habríamos telefoneado
telefonearías	telefonearíais	habrías telefoneado	habríais telefoneado
telefonearía	telefonearían	habría telefoneado	habrían telefoneado

6　presente de subjuntivo

		13　perfecto de subjuntivo	
telefonee	telefoneemos	haya telefoneado	hayamos telefoneado
telefonees	telefoneéis	hayas telefoneado	hayáis telefoneado
telefonee	telefoneen	haya telefoneado	hayan telefoneado

7　imperfecto de subjuntivo

		14　pluscuamperfecto de subjuntivo	
telefoneara	telefoneáramos	hubiera telefoneado	hubiéramos telefoneado
telefonearas	telefonearais	hubieras telefoneado	hubierais telefoneado
telefoneara	telefonearan	hubiera telefoneado	hubieran telefoneado
OR		OR	
telefonease	telefoneásemos	hubiese telefoneado	hubiésemos telefoneado
telefoneases	telefoneaseis	hubieses telefoneado	hubieseis telefoneado
telefonease	telefoneasen	hubiese telefoneado	hubiesen telefoneado

imperativo

—	telefoneemos
telefonea; no telefonees	telefonead; no telefoneéis
telefonee	telefoneen

Words and expressions related to this verb

el teléfono　telephone
telefonista　telephone operator
telefónico, telefónica　telephonic
marcar el número de teléfono　to dial
　a telephone number

la guía telefónica　telephone book
la cabina telefónica　telephone booth
el número de teléfono　telephone number
por teléfono　by telephone

tener

to have, to hold

Gerundio **teniendo**   Part. pas. **tenido**

The Seven Simple Tenses	
Singular	Plural

The Seven Compound Tenses	
Singular	Plural

1   presente de indicativo

tengo	tenemos
tienes	tenéis
tiene	tienen

8   perfecto de indicativo

he tenido	hemos tenido
has tenido	habéis tenido
ha tenido	han tenido

2   imperfecto de indicativo

tenía	teníamos
tenías	teníais
tenía	tenían

9   pluscuamperfecto de indicativo

había tenido	habíamos tenido
habías tenido	habíais tenido
había tenido	habían tenido

3   pretérito

tuve	tuvimos
tuviste	tuvisteis
tuvo	tuvieron

10   pretérito anterior

hube tenido	hubimos tenido
hubiste tenido	hubisteis tenido
hubo tenido	hubieron tenido

4   futuro

tendré	tendremos
tendrás	tendréis
tendrá	tendrán

11   futuro perfecto

habré tenido	habremos tenido
habrás tenido	habréis tenido
habrá tenido	habrán tenido

5   potencial simple

tendría	tendríamos
tendrías	tendríais
tendría	tendrían

12   potencial compuesto

habría tenido	habríamos tenido
habrías tenido	habríais tenido
habría tenido	habrían tenido

6   presente de subjuntivo

tenga	tengamos
tengas	tengáis
tenga	tengan

13   perfecto de subjuntivo

haya tenido	hayamos tenido
hayas tenido	hayáis tenido
haya tenido	hayan tenido

7   imperfecto de subjuntivo

tuviera	tuviéramos
tuvieras	tuvierais
tuviera	tuvieran
OR	
tuviese	tuviésemos
tuvieses	tuvieseis
tuviese	tuviesen

14   pluscuamperfecto de subjuntivo

hubiera tenido	hubiéramos tenido
hubieras tenido	hubierais tenido
hubiera tenido	hubieran tenido
OR	
hubiese tenido	hubiésemos tenido
hubieses tenido	hubieseis tenido
hubiese tenido	hubiesen tenido

imperativo

—	tengamos
ten; no tengas	tened; no tengáis
tenga	tengan

Common idiomatic expressions using this verb

Anda despacio que tengo prisa. Make haste slowly.
tener prisa   to be in a hurry
tener hambre   to be hungry
tener sed   to be thirsty

tener frío   to be (feel) cold (persons)
tener calor   to be (feel) warm (persons)
retener   to retain

vivir

to live

Gerundio **viviendo** Part. pas. **vivido**

The Seven Simple Tenses	
Singular	Plural

The Seven Compound Tenses	
Singular	Plural

1 presente de indicativo

Singular	Plural
vivo	vivimos
vives	vivís
vive	viven

8 perfecto de indicativo

Singular	Plural
he vivido	hemos vivido
has vivido	habéis vivido
ha vivido	han vivido

2 imperfecto de indicativo

Singular	Plural
vivía	vivíamos
vivías	vivíais
vivía	vivían

9 pluscuamperfecto de indicativo

Singular	Plural
había vivido	habíamos vivido
habías vivido	habíais vivido
había vivido	habían vivido

3 pretérito

Singular	Plural
viví	vivimos
viviste	vivisteis
vivió	vivieron

10 pretérito anterior

Singular	Plural
hube vivido	hubimos vivido
hubiste vivido	hubisteis vivido
hubo vivido	hubieron vivido

4 futuro

Singular	Plural
viviré	viviremos
vivirás	viviréis
vivirá	vivirán

11 futuro perfecto

Singular	Plural
habré vivido	habremos vivido
habrás vivido	habréis vivido
habrá vivido	habrán vivido

5 potencial simple

Singular	Plural
viviría	viviríamos
vivirías	viviríais
viviría	vivirían

12 potencial compuesto

Singular	Plural
habría vivido	habríamos vivido
habrías vivido	habríais vivido
habría vivido	habrían vivido

6 presente de subjuntivo

Singular	Plural
viva	vivamos
vivas	viváis
viva	vivan

13 perfecto de subjuntivo

Singular	Plural
haya vivido	hayamos vivido
hayas vivido	hayáis vivido
haya vivido	hayan vivido

7 imperfecto de subjuntivo

Singular	Plural
viviera	viviéramos
vivieras	vivierais
viviera	vivieran
OR	
viviese	viviésemos
vivieses	vivieseis
viviese	viviesen

14 pluscuamperfecto de subjuntivo

Singular	Plural
hubiera vivido	hubiéramos vivido
hubieras vivido	hubierais vivido
hubiera vivido	hubieran vivido
OR	
hubiese vivido	hubiésemos vivido
hubieses vivido	hubieseis vivido
hubiese vivido	hubiesen vivido

imperativo

—	vivamos
vive; no vivas	vivid; no viváis
viva	vivan

Words and expressions related to this verb

vivir de to live on
la vida life
en vida while living, while alive
ganarse la vida to earn one's living

vivir del aire to live on thin air
vivir para ver to live and learn
vivir a oscuras to live in ignorance
revivir to revive

Verbs
used in this book

◆

1. **abrir,** to open
2. **acabar,** to finish
3. **acercarse,** to approach
4. **acostarse,** to go to bed
5. **acostumbrar,** to be in the habit of
6. **alegrarse,** to be glad
7. **almorzar,** to have lunch
8. **aprender,** to learn
9. **asistir,** to attend
10. **bailar,** to dance
11. **bajar,** to go down
12. **beber,** to drink
13. **buscar,** to look for
14. **caer,** to fall down
15. **caerse,** to fall
16. **cantar,** to sing
17. **casarse,** to get married
18. **cerrar,** to close
19. **comenzar,** to begin
20. **comer,** to eat
21. **comprar,** to buy
22. **comprender,** to understand
23. **conocer,** to know
24. **contestar,** to answer
25. **copiar,** to copy
26. **costar,** to cost
27. **cruzar,** to cross
28. **cumplir,** to reach (a birthday)
29. **dar,** to give
30. **decir,** to say, tell
31. **dedicarse,** to devote oneself
32. **descansar,** to rest
33. **detenerse,** to stop
34. **divertirse,** to have a good time
35. **echar,** to throw
36. **empezar,** to begin, start
37. **emplear,** to use, employ
38. **encontrarse,** to be, find oneself (relating to health)
39. **enfadarse,** to get angry
40. **enseñar,** to teach, show
41. **entrar,** to enter, go in
42. **escribir,** to write
43. **escuchar,** to listen (to)
44. **estar,** to be
45. **estudiar,** to study
46. **faltar,** to lack, need
47. **ganar,** to earn, win, gain

48. **gozar,** to enjoy
49. **gustar,** to please
50. **haber,** to have (auxiliary)
51. **hablar,** to talk, speak
52. **hacer,** to make, do
53. **herir,** to injure, wound
54. **ir,** to go
55. **irse,** to go away
56. **jugar,** to play (a game)
57. **lavarse,** to wash oneself
58. **leer,** to read
59. **levantarse,** to get up
60. **limpiar,** to clean
61. **llamar,** to call
62. **llamarse,** to be called, named
63. **llegar,** to arrive
64. **llorar,** to cry, weep
65. **llover,** to rain
66. **mencionar,** to mention
67. **nacer,** to be born
68. **necesitar,** to need
69. **nevar,** to snow
70. **olvidarse,** to forget
71. **pagar,** to pay
72. **parecerse,** to be alike, look alike
73. **pasar,** to pass, spend (time)
74. **pasearse,** to take a ride
75. **pedir,** to ask (for)
76. **peinarse,** to comb one's hair
77. **pensar,** to think
78. **poder,** to be able, can
79. **poner,** to put, place
80. **ponerse,** to put on
81. **preferir,** to prefer
82. **preparar,** to prepare
83. **prepararse,** to get ready
84. **prestar,** to lend
85. **quedarse,** to remain
86. **querer,** to wish, want
87. **recibir,** to receive
88. **reírse,** to laugh
89. **romperse,** to break
90. **saber,** to know
91. **salir,** to leave, go out
92. **seguir,** to follow, continue
93. **sentir,** to regret, feel sorry
94. **sentirse,** to feel
95. **ser,** to be

96. **soñar,** to dream
97. **subir,** to go up
98. **tener,** to have, hold
99. **terminar,** to finish, end
100. **tocar,** to play (instrument)
101. **tomar,** to take
102. **trabajar,** to work

103. **traducir,** to translate
104. **tratar,** to try
105. **vender,** to sell
106. **venir,** to come
107. **ver,** to see
108. **vestirse,** to get dressed
109. **volver,** to return, go back

Numbers

Cardinal numbers: zero to one hundred million

0 cero
1 uno, una
2 dos
3 tres
4 cuatro
5 cinco
6 seis
7 siete
8 ocho
9 nueve
10 diez
11 once
12 doce
13 trece
14 catorce
15 quince
16 diez y seis or **dieciséis**
17 diez y siete or **diecisiete**
18 diez y ocho or **dieciocho**
19 diez y nueve or **diecinueve**
20 veinte
21 veinte y uno or veintiuno
22 veinte y dos or veintidós
23 veinte y tres or veintitrés
24 veinte y cuatro or veinticuatro
25 veinte y cinco or veinticinco
26 veinte y seis or veintiséis
27 veinte y siete or veintisiete
28 veinte y ocho or veintiocho
29 veinte y nueve or veintinueve
30 treinta
31 treinta y uno, treinta y una

32 treinta y dos, *etc.*
40 cuarenta
41 cuarenta y uno, cuarenta y una
42 cuarenta y dos, *etc.*
50 cincuenta
51 cincuenta y uno, cincuenta y una
52 cincuenta y dos, *etc.*
60 sesenta
61 sesenta y uno, sesenta y una
62 sesenta y dos, *etc.*
70 setenta
71 setenta y uno, setenta y una
72 setenta y dos, *etc.*
80 ochenta
81 ochenta y uno, ochenta y una
82 ochenta y dos, *etc.*
90 noventa
91 noventa y uno, noventa y una
92 noventa y dos, *etc.*
100 ciento (cien)
101 ciento uno, ciento una
102 ciento dos, *etc.*
200 doscientos, doscientas
300 trescientos, trescientas
400 cuatrocientos, cuatrocientas

500 quinientos, quinientas
600 seiscientos, seiscientas
700 setecientos, setecientas
800 ochocientos, ochocientas
900 novecientos, novecientas
1,000 mil
2,000 dos mil
3,000 tres mil, *etc.*
100,000 cien mil
200,000 doscientos mil, doscientas mil
300,000 trescientos mil, trescientas mil, *etc.*
1,000,000 un millón (de + noun)
2,000,000 dos millones (de + noun)
3,000,000 tres millones (de + noun), *etc.*
100,000,000 cien millones (de + noun)

Approximate numbers

unos veinte libros, about (some) twenty books
unas treinta personas, about (some) thirty persons

Simple arithmetical expressions

dos **y** dos son cuatro	2 + 2 = 4	tres **por** cinco son quince	3 × 5 = 15
diez **menos** cinco son cinco	10 − 5 = 5	diez **dividido por** dos son cinco	10 − 2 = 5

Ordinal numbers: first to tenth

primero, primer, primera	first	1st	**sexto, sexta**	sixth	6th
segundo, segunda	second	2nd	**séptimo, séptima**	seventh	7th
tercero, tercer, tercera	third	3rd	**octavo, octava**	eighth	8th
cuarto, cuarta	fourth	4th	**noveno, novena**	ninth	9th
quinto, quinta	fifth	5th	**décimo, décima**	tenth	10th

Note

that beyond 10th the cardinal numbers are used instead of the ordinal numbers, but when there is a noun involved, the cardinal number is placed after the noun: **el día 15** (**el día quince,** the fifteenth day).

Note

also that in titles of monarchs, *etc.* the definite article is not used between the person's name and the number, but it is in English: **Alfonso XIII** (**Alfonso Trece,** Alfonso the Thirteenth).

And note

that **noveno** (9th) changes to **nono** in such titles: **Luis IX** (**Luis Nono,** Louis the Ninth).

Index of idioms, verbal expressions, proverbs and key words showing their location in this book

The location number given is the *Tarea* number. The abbreviation RT plus a number is the Review Test number.

a eso de 38
a la derecha 8
a la izquierda 8
a las tres 7
a lo largo de 15
a media voz 23
a menudo 16
a propósito 34
a qué hora . . . 7
a tiempo 19
a veces 11
al (+ inf.) 10
al campo 4
al centro 16
al instante 33
al lado de 11
al otro lado de la calle 24, RT 8
al principio 30
acabar de (+ inf.) 22
acercarse a 32, RT 11
acostarse 13
acostumbrar (+ inf.) 5
adiós 40
Ahí tiene Ud. . . . 8
ahora mismo 10
alegrarse de 37
algunas veces 16
antes de (+ inf.) 12
apenas 25
aprender a (+ inf.) 21
aprender de memoria 35, RT 12
Aquí tiene Ud. . . . 8
asistir a 26
ayer por la tarde 23
bajar la escalera 25
bastante bien 36
casarse con alguien 26
cerca de 6
comenzar a (+ inf.) 21
¡cómo no! 14
¿Cómo se dice . . . 40
conocer 34

Cuando el gato va a sus devociones, bailan los ratones. RT 13
cumplir . . . años 31
dar a 1
dar de comer a 15
dar las gracias a alguien 31
dar un paseo 3
de buena gana 24, RT 8
de madrugada 13
de más en más 28
de nada 40
de noche 27, RT 9
de nuevo 36
de ordinario 19
¿de qué color . . . 23
¿de quién . . . 24, RT 8
de repente 33, RT 11
de vez en cuando 11
dedicarse a 39
dentro de ocho días 37
dentro de poco 35
dentro de quince días 37
descansar 28
detenerse 32, RT 11
Dicho y hecho. RT 2
echar de menos 36
El ejercicio hace maestro al novicio. RT 8
El que no se aventura no cruza el mar. RT 12
El tiempo da buen consejo. RT 7
en casa 3
en lugar de 22
en punto 26
en seguida 33, RT 11
en voz alta 9
en voz baja 9
encontrarse 29, RT 10
enfadarse 33, RT 11
enfrente de 19
enseñar a (+ inf.) 18
entrar en (+ noun) 5

Es la una. 7
¡Eso es una lástima! 29, RT 10
esta noche 17, RT 6
estar bien 4
estar cansado(a) 28
estar de pie 23
estar enfermo(a) 4
estar mejor 4
estar situado(a) 11
faltarle algo a alguien 30
finalmente 30
fue una ganga 24, RT 8
gozar de 15
había 26
hace dos años que (+ pres. tense) 18
hace sol 3
hacer buen tiempo 2
hacer calor 2, RT 5
hacer fresco 2
hacer frío 2, RT 5
hacer las maletas 13
hacer lo mejor posible 18
hacer preguntas 18
hacer un tiempo agradable 2
hacer un viaje 13
hacer una visita 22
hacerse daño 25
Hágame el favor de (+ inf.) 14
hasta la vista 34
hasta luego 40
hay 6
hay que (+ inf.) 8
hay sol 3
herir 29, RT 10
hoy día 39
ir a buscar 31
ir de compras 30
irse 37
jugar a la pelota 6
jugar al tenis 6
la semana pasada 25

la semana que viene   10
lavarse   12
levantarse   1
limpiarse los dientes   12
Lo siento.   17, RT 6
llamar a la puerta   38
llamarse   1
llegar a ser   39
llegar tarde   26
llover   3
Más vale pájaro en mano que ciento volando.   RT 4
Más vale tarde que nunca.   RT 3
me gusta (+ inf.)   6
me gustaría (+ inf.)   22
Mientras hay alma hay esperanza.   RT 10
muchas gracias   40
muchas veces   19
Mucho ruido y pocas nueces.   RT 5
necesitar   21
nevar   3
no (+ verb) nada   20, RT 7
no (+ verb) nadie   20, RT 7
no (+ verb) ninguno (ningún)   20, RT 7
no (+ verb) nunca   20, RT 7
olvidarse de (+ inf.)   34
para (+ inf.)   27, RT 9
parecerse a   22
pasar un buen rato   15
pasar una semana   4
pasearse en automóvil   10

pedirle algo a alguien   30
peinarse   12
pensar (+ inf.)   10
pensar de   35, RT 12
pensar en   35, RT 12
Piedra movediza, el moho no la cobija.   RT 11
poner la mesa   11
ponerse   33, RT 11
ponerse a (+ inf.)   32, RT 11
por allá   24, RT 8
por ejemplo   16
por la tarde   16
por lo general   39
por supuesto   27, RT 9
por todas partes   31
prepararse a (+ inf.)   36
prepararse para (+ inf.)   36
prestar atención   21
¿Qué hora es?   7
¿Qué pasó?   29, RT 10
¿Qué tal?   36
¿Qué tienes, Miguel?   17
querer a alguien   31
querer decir   40
Quien canta su mal espanta.   RT 6
quitarse   14
reírse a carcajadas   23
romperse   25
saber (+ inf.)   9
salir de   32, RT 11
se dice   39
seguir (+ gerund)   18
sentirse bien   28

ser hora de (+ inf.)   21
Si a Roma fueres, haz como vieres.   RT 9
sin duda   32
Son las dos.   7
soñar con   37
subir la escalera   38
Tal padre, tal hijo   RT 1
tener ... años   1
tener buena cara   17, RT 6
tener calor   14, RT 5
tener cita   7
tener dolor de cabeza   17, RT 6
tener frío   14, RT 5
tener ganas de (+ inf.)   5
tener hambre   5
tener miedo   27, RT 9
tener que (+ inf.)   13
tener razón   27, RT 9
tener sed   5
tener tiempo de (+ inf.)   35
tocar el piano   15
tocarle a uno   9
todas las mañanas   1
todo el día   28
todo el mundo   29, RT 10
tratar de (+ inf.)   38
un poco de   38
una vez más   34
unas veces   19
¡Vamos a ver!   9
vestirse   12
ya no   20, RT 7

Vocabulary
Spanish and English Words
in one alphabetical listing

◆

This list of vocabulary contains words and expressions in Spanish and English in one alphabetical order because I think it is convenient if you look in one place instead of two for an entry. One listing prevents you from looking inadvertently in a Spanish listing for an English word or in an English listing for a Spanish word. Also, cognates and near-cognates in both languages are reduced to a single entry. All Spanish words are printed in bold face.

The preposition *to* in an English infinitive is omitted, e.g., *to go* is listed under *go*.

If you do not understand the meaning of an abbreviation, look it up in the list of abbreviations here below. Entries in this vocabulary pertain to words used in this book. For any not listed here, consult a standard Spanish-English/English-Spanish dictionary.

Abbreviations

abs. absolute
adj. adjective
adv. adverb
art. article
aux. auxiliary (helping)
ca. circa, about, around + year
cf. compare
cond. conditional
conj. conjunction
def. definite
dem. demonstrative
dir. direct
ed. edition
EE.UU. Estados Unidos
e.g. for example
etc. and so on, and so forth
excl. exclamation
f., fem. feminine

fam. familiar
ff. and the following
fut. future
i.e. that is, that is to say
imper. imperative
imperf. imperfect
indef. indefinite
indic. indicative
indir. indirect
interj. interjection
m., masc. masculine
n. noun
neg. negative
neut. neuter
num. numeral, number
obj. object
part. participle
perf. perfect

pers. person
pl. plural
pluperf. pluperfect
poss. possessive
prep. preposition
pres. present
pret. preterit
prog. progressive
pron. pronoun
refl. reflexive
rel. relative
s., sing. singular
sub. subjunctive
subj. subject
superl. superlative
Ud. (vd.) usted (you, sing., polite)
Uds. (vds.) ustedes (you, pl., polite)
v. verb

A

a *prep.,* at, to; **a menudo,** often; **a la una,** at one o'clock; **a las dos,** at two o'clock

able, to be *v.,* **poder**

accept *v.,* **aceptar;** I can't accept, **no puedo aceptar**

acostarse *refl. v.,* to go to bed; **yo me acuesto a las once,** I go to bed at eleven o'clock

actor, **el actor;** actress, **la actriz**

acuerdo *n.m.,* agreement; **de acuerdo,** okay, agreed

adiós, good-bye

¿adónde? *adv.,* where? where to?

adulto *n.m.,* adult

agradable *adj.,* pleasant, nice, agreeable

agua *n.f.,* water; **el agua fresca,** cold (fresh) water

ahora *adv.,* now

air mail, **el correo aéreo;** airplane, **el avión**

al *contraction of* **a + el,** to (at) the; **voy al cine,** I'm going to the cinema; **hablo al profesor,** I'm talking to the teacher; **al mismo tiempo,** at the same time

alemán *n.m.,* German (language)

algo *pron.,* something

alguien *pron.,* somebody, someone

alma *n.m.,* soul

almorzar *v.,* to lunch, to have lunch; **almuerzo a la una,** I have lunch at one o'clock; **almuerzo** *n.m.,* lunch; **este almuerzo es bueno,** this lunch is good

also *adv.,* **también**

always *adv.,* **siempre;** see Synonyms and Antonyms in the Appendix

amigo *n.m.,* **amiga** *n.f.,* friend

and *conj.,* **y** or **e;** normally use **y** to mean and; use **e** if the word right after it begins with **i** or stressed **hi; e interesante,** and interesting; **hijos e hijas,** sons and daughters

año *n.m.,* year

anything *pron.,* **algo;** not anything (nothing), **nada**

apartamento *n.m.,* apartment

appointment, **la cita**

April, abril *n.m.*

aprender *v.,* to learn

arrive *v.,* **llegar**

arroz *n.m.,* rice

aspirin, **la aspirina**

at *prep.,* **a;** see the entry **a** in this list

atentamente *adv.,* attentively, politely (in business letters, sincerely yours, yours very truly)

audience, **la audiencia, el auditorio público**

August, **agosto** *n.m.*

aunt, **la tía**

autumn, **el otoño**

avenida *n.f.,* avenue

aventurarse *refl. v.,* to venture, to set out on an adventure

B

bacon, **el tocino**

bag, **el saco**

bailar *v.,* to dance

balcón *n.m.,* balcony

ball, **la pelota**

bank, **el banco**

baño *n.m.,* bath; **el cuarto de baño,** bathroom

bargain, **una ganga**

bathroom, **el cuarto de baño**

beach, **la playa;** I like the beach, **me gusta la playa**

bean, **el frijol; los frijoles**

beber *v.,* to drink; **bebo agua cuando tengo sed** I drink water when I'm thirsty

because *conj.,* **porque**

bed, **la cama**

begin *v.,* **empezar;** see the 22 verbs in the Appendix

bello, bella, bellos, bellas *adj.,* beautiful, handsome; see Antonyms in the Appendix

better, best *adj., adv.,* **mejor;** see Synonyms and Antonyms in the Appendix

bien *adv.,* well; opposite is **mal** badly; see Antonyms in the Appendix

billete *n.m.,* ticket

birthday, **el cumpleaños**

bizcocho *n.m.,* cake

boat, **un barco;** ship, **un paquebote, un vapor**

book, **el libro**

boots, **las botas**

boy, **el muchacho, el chico;** little boy, **el chiquito**

bread, **el pan**

breakfast, **el desayuno;** to have breakfast, **desayunar**

bring *v.,* **traer;** I brought the ice cream, **yo traje el helado**

brother, **el hermano**

buen, bueno, buena, buenos, buenas *adj.,* good; **un buen libro,** a good book; **el desayuno es bueno,** the breakfast is good; **una buena vista,** a good view; see Antonyms in the Appendix

bus, **el autobús**
but *conj.*, **pero**
butter, **la mantequilla**
buy *v.*, **comprar**
by *prep.* **por**

C

cabeza *n.f.*, head; **tengo dolor de cabeza,** I have a headache
cake, **el bizcocho, el pastel**
calefacción *n.f.*, heating (in a house, apartment)
calle *n.f.*, street
camping, to go *v.*, **ir de camping**
campo *n.m.*, countryside
can, be able to *v.*, **poder**
cantar *v.*, to sing
car, **el coche, el carro, el automóvil;** a car accident, **un accidente de coche**
cariño *n.m.*, affection; **con cariño,** affectionately
carta *n.f.*, letter; **escribo una carta,** I'm writing a letter
casa *n.f.*, house; **en casa,** at home
cat, **el gato**
catorce, fourteen; see Numbers in the Appendix
celery, **el apio**
cena *n.f.*, dinner
cerca de *adv.*, near
cereal, **el cereal**
chair, **la silla**
cheese, **el queso**
chicken, **el pollo**
chico *n.m.*, boy; **chiquito,** little boy
child, **el niño, la niña**
chop, **la chuleta;** pork chops, **las chuletas de cerdo**
ciento, one hundred; see Numbers in the Appendix
cinco, five; see Numbers in the Appendix
cinema, **el cine;** I'm going to the movies, **voy al cine**
cita *n.f.*, appointment, date (with a person)
ciudad *n.f.*, city
clase *n.f.*, class
close *v.*, **cerrar;** see Antonyms in the Appendix
closet, **el armario**
clothes, clothing, **la ropa**
clothes dryer, **la secadora de ropa**
coat, **el abrigo**
cobijar *v.*, to cover
cocina *n.f.*, kitchen

coffee, **el café**
come *v.*, **venir;** I'm coming to the party, **yo vengo a la fiesta;** next week, **la semana que viene;** next month, **el mes que viene**
comenzar *v.*, to begin, to start, to commence
comer *v.*, to eat
como *adv., conj.*, how, as; **¿cómo está Ud.?** how are you? **¿cómo se llama Ud.?** what is your name? **¡haz como quieres!** do as you want!
comprar *v.*, to buy, to purchase; **compré, compró** *pret. (past) tense;* **yo compré una camisa,** I bought a shirt; **María compró zapatos,** Mary bought shoes
con *prep.*, with
coñcert, el concierto; at a concert, **a un concierto**
consejo *n.m.*, advice, counsel
contestar *v.*, to answer, to reply
cook *v.*, **cocinar;** the cook, **el cocinero, la cocinera**
corn, **el maíz**
correo *n.m.*, mail; **correo aéreo,** air mail
correr *v.*, to run; **corren,** they are running
cosa *n.f.*, thing
costar *v.*, to cost
countryside, **el campo;** to the countryside, **al campo**
cousin, **el primo, la prima**
cream, **la crema**
cruzar *v.*, to cross
cuaderno *n.m.*, notebook
cual, cuales *pron.*, what, which
cuando *adv.*, when
cuanto, cuanta, cuantos, cuantas *adj.*, how much, how many; **¿cuánto dinero?** how much money? **¿cuánto cuesta?** how much does it cost? **¿cuántos libros?** how many books? **¿cuántos años tienes (tú)?** how old are you?
cuarto *n.m.*, room; **el cuarto de baño,** bathroom
cup, **la taza;** a cup of coffee, **una taza de café;** a cup of tea, **una taza de té**

D

dar *v.*, to give; see review of basic Spanish idioms with **dar** and the 22 verbs in the Appendix
dance *v.*, **bailar**
dare *v.*, **osar;** they dared, **osaron**
dark haired person, **el moreno, la morena**
daughter, **la hija**
day, **el día;** daytime, **de día;** during the day, **durante el día**

de *prep.*, from, of

December, **diciembre** *n.m.*

decir *v.*, to say, to tell; see the 22 verbs in the Appendix

del *contraction of* **de + el,** of the, from the; **del cine** from the movies; **del parque** from the park

desayuno *n.m.*, breakfast

desear *v.*, to desire, to want

dessert, **el postre**

devociones *n.f.*, *pl.*, prayers

día *n.m.*, day

difficult *adj.*, **difícil**

dining room, **el comedor**

dinner, **la cena;** to dine, have dinner *v.*, **cenar**

Dios, God; **adiós,** good-bye

dirección *n.f.*, address, direction

dirty *adj.*, **sucio, sucia, sucios, sucias; tú tienes las manos sucias,** you have dirty hands

do *v.*, **hacer;** see the 22 verbs in the Appendix; do you have? **¿tiene Ud.? (¿tienes tú?)**

doctor, **el doctor, la doctora; el médico**

dog, **el perro**

dolor *n.m.*, ache, pain

donde *adv.*, where

dormitorio *n.m.*, bedroom

dos, two; see Numbers in the Appendix

dress, **el vestido;** to dress oneself *refl. v.*, **vestirse;** I get dressed, **yo me visto;** he hasn't finished dressing (himself), **no ha terminado de vestirse**

drink *v.*, **beber;** the child is drinking milk, **el niño bebe leche;** I drink milk, **yo bebo leche**

drug store, **la farmacia**

dryer (clothes), **la secadora de ropa**

durante *adv.*, during

E

e *conj.*, and; see the entry *and* in this list

each *adj.*, **cada;** each boy, **cada muchacho;** each girl, **cada muchacha**

early *adv.*, **temprano**

easy *adj.*, **fácil**

eat *v.*, **comer;** I eat, **yo como;** I ate, **yo comí**

EE.UU., *abbreviation of* **Estados Unidos** (United States)

egg, **el huevo**

ejemplar *n.m.*, sample

ejercicio *n.m.*, exercise

él *pron.*, *m.s.*, he, him; **él está enfermo,** he is sick; **con él,** with him

el *def. art.*, *m.s.*, the; **el chico,** the boy; *pl.*, **los chicos; el que ...,** he who ...

elect *v.*, **elegir;** he elected, **él eligió**

electricidad *n.f.*, electricity

ella *pron.*, *f.s.*, she, her; **con ella,** with her; **ella que ...,** she who ...

ellas *pron.*, *f. pl.*, they, them; **con ellas,** with them

ellos *pron.*, *m. pl.*, they, them; **con ellos,** with them

empezar *v.*, to begin, to start, to commence; see the 22 verbs in the Appendix

en *prep.*, in, at; **en casa,** at home; **en este momento,** at this moment

end *v.*, **terminar**

English (language), **el inglés**

enjoy oneself *refl. v.*, **divertirse;** I am enjoying myself, **yo me divierto**

enseñar *v.*, to teach

entender *v.*, to understand

enviar *v.*, to send; **enviarme,** to send me

escribir *v.*, to write; see the 22 verbs in the Appendix

escuchar *v.*, to listen (to)

eso *neuter pron.*, that; **¡eso es una lástima!** that's too bad!

español (language) *n.m.*, Spanish

espantar *v.*, to chase away

esperanza *n.f.*, hope

esta *demons. adj. f., s.*, this; **esta papelería,** this stationery shop; **esta casa,** this house

estación *n.f.*, season; station

Estados Unidos (EE.UU.) *n.m.*, *pl.*, United States (U.S.)

estar *v.* to be; see review of basic Spanish idioms with **estar** and the 22 verbs in the Appendix

este *demons. adj., m., s.*, this; **este medicamento,** this medicine; **en este momento,** at this moment

estimado señor, dear sir; **estimada señora,** dear madam

esto *neuter pron.*, this; **¿qué es esto?** what is this?

estudiante *n., m.f.*, student: **María es estudiante,** Mary is a student; **Roberto es estudiante,** Robert is a student

estudiar *v.*, to study; see the 22 verbs in the Appendix

evening, **la noche;** every evening, **todas las noches**

every day, **todos los días;** every morning, **todas las mañanas**

excelente *adj.*, excellent

expensive *adj.*, **caro, cara, caros, caras**

extraordinario *adj.*, extraordinary

F

fácil *adj.,* easy; *pl.,* **fáciles**

fall (season of the year), **el otoño**

family, **la familia**

fat *adj.,* **gordo, gorda, gordos, gordas**

father, **el padre**

faucet, **el grifo**

February, **febrero** *n.m.*

fecha *n.f.,* date (of the week)

feel better (health), **estar mejor;** I'm feeling
   better, **estoy mejor;** see the review of basic
   Spanish idioms with **estar** in the Appendix

fever, **la fiebre**

fifty-two, **cincuenta y dos;** see Numbers in the
   Appendix

finish *v.,* **terminar, completar**

first *adj.,* **primero, primera**

fish, **el pez, el pescado; los peces, los pescados**

flor *n.f.,* flower

fly *v.,* **volar**

fontanería *n.f.,* plumbing fixtures; **la plomería**

for *prep.,* **para**

forget *v.,* **olvidar;** he forgot, **él olvidó**

forty, **cuarenta;** see Numbers in the Appendix

fourteen, **catorce;** see Numbers in the
   Appendix

francés *n.m.,* French (language)

friend, **un amigo, una amiga**

from *prep.,* **de**

fruta *n.f.,* fruit

fue, fui, fuiste *v. forms of* **ir** and **ser;** see **ir** and
   ser in the Appendix

funny *adj.,* **cómico**

G

gana *n.f.,* desire; **tengo ganas de comer,** I feel
   like eating

garden, **el jardín**

gato *n.m.,* cat

generalmente *adv.,* generally

German (language), **el alemán**

get up *refl. v.,* **levantarse;** I get up at six o'clock,
   Yo me levanto a las seis

girl, **la muchacha, la chica**

go *v.,* **ir;** see the 22 verbs in the Appendix

go on a trip *v.,* **hacer un viaje;** see the review of
   basic Spanish idioms with **hacer** and the 22
   verbs in the Appendix

go to bed *refl. v.,* **acostarse;** I go to bed at ten
   o'clock **Yo me acuesto a las diez**

God, **Dios**

goma *n.f.,* gum, rubber; **la goma de borrar**
   eraser

good *adj.,* **buen, bueno, buena, buenos, buenas;**
   a good book, **un buen libro;** this book is
   good, **este libro es bueno;** see Antonyms in
   the Appendix

good-bye, **adiós**

gran, grande *adj.,* large, big; **un gran libro,** a
   big book; **una casa grande,** a big house; **un
   perro grande,** a big dog; see Antonyms and
   Synonyms in the Appendix

grave *adj.,* serious

guitar, **la guitarra**

gustar *v.,* to be pleasing (to), to please; **me gusta
   el helado,** I like ice cream; **¿le gusta a Ud.?**
   do you like?

H

h. *abbreviation for* **hora,** hour

hablar *v.,* to speak, to talk; see the 22 verbs in
   the Appendix

hacer *v.,* to do, to make; see the review of basic
   Spanish idioms with **hacer** and the 22 verbs
   in the Appendix

hágame el favor, please

hair, **el cabello, el pelo**

ham, **el jamón**

hambre *n.f.,* hunger; **tengo hambre,** I'm hungry

hand, **la mano**

handsome *adj.,* **guapo**

happy *adj.,* **contento, contenta, contentos,
   contentas;** see Antonyms and Synonyms in
   the Appendix

hasta *adv.,* until; **hasta la vista,** see you later;
   hasta pronto, see you soon

have *v.,* **tener; tengo una bicicleta,** I have a
   bicycle; **tener que,** to have to; **tengo que
   estudiar ahora,** I have to study now; **haber,**
   to have (as an auxiliary, helping verb to form
   the compound tenses); see the review of basic
   Spanish idioms with **tener** in the Appendix;
   see also **haber** and **tener** among the 22 verbs
   in the Appendix

hay, there is, there are

he *pron.,* **él**

head, **la cabeza;** headache, **un dolor de cabeza**

hear *v.,* **oír**

heart, **el corazón**

heating system, **la calefacción**

here *adv.,* **aquí**

hermana *n.f.,* sister

hermano *n.m.,* brother; **hermanos,** brothers, brothers and sisters

hija *n.f.,* daughter; **hijo,** *n.m.* son

him *pron.,* **él;** with him, **con él;** for him, **para él**

hold, *v.,* **tener**

home, **la casa,** at my home (house), **en mi casa**

hora *n.f.,* hour (time); **¿qué hora es?** what time is it?

horses, **los caballos**

hour, **la hora**

house, **la casa**

how *adv.,* **como;** how many, how much, **cuanto, cuanta, cuantos, cuantas; ¿cuántos años tiene Ud.?** how old are you?

hoy *adv.,* today

hunger, **la hambre;** I'm hungry, **tengo hambre**

hurry *refl. v.,* **apresurarse;** I'm hurrying, **yo me apresuro**

husband, **el marido**

if *conj.,* **si**

I'm sorry, **lo siento**

in *prep.,* **en;** to be in love, **estar enamorado(a);** they are in love, **están enamorados**

inglés *n.m.,* English (language)

intelligent *adj.,* **inteligente**

interesting *adj.,* **interesante**

invierno *n.m.,* winter

invitar *v.,* to invite; see the 22 verbs in the Appendix

invitation, **la invitación**

ir *v.,* to go; see the 22 verbs in the Appendix

is there . . . ? **¿hay . . . ?**

it is one o'clock, **es la una;** it is two thirty, **son las dos y media**

italiano *n.m.,* Italian (language)

it's cold today, **hace frío hoy**

it's sunny today, **hace sol hoy**

it's warm today, **hace calor hoy**

I

I *pron.,* **yo**

I am feeling better, **estoy mejor;** see the review of basic Spanish idioms with **estar** and the 22 verbs in the Appendix

I am going to the movies (cinema), **yo voy al cine;** see the verb **ir** among the 22 verbs in the Appendix

I am tired, **estoy cansado (cansada);** see the review of basic Spanish idioms with **estar** and the 22 verbs in the Appendix

I drink, **yo bebo**

I feel sick, **estoy enfermo (enferma);** see the review of basic Spanish idioms with **estar** and the 22 verbs in the Appendix

I get up, **yo me levanto**

I go to bed, **yo me acuesto;** to go to bed **acostarse**

I have, **yo tengo;** see **tener** among the 22 verbs in the Appendix

I hurt myself yesterday, **yo me hice daño ayer**

I like, **me gusta (gustan);** see **gustar** in this list; I like Spanish, **me gusta el español**

I read in Spanish, **leo en español**

I see nobody, **yo no veo a nadie**

I study Spanish, **yo estudio español**

I walk, **yo ando, yo marcho, yo voy a pie;** see **ir** among the 22 verbs in the Appendix

I would like, **me gustaría, quisiera**

I write in Spanish, **escribo en español**

ice cream, **el helado**

idioma *n.m.,* language

J

January, **enero** *n.m.*

jugar *v.,* to play; **juego al tenis,** I play tennis; **juego a la pelota,** I play ball

July, **julio** *n.m.*

June, **junio** *n.m.*

K

king, **el rey**

kitchen, **la cocina**

know (how) *v.,* **saber;** I know how to play the guitar, **yo sé tocar la guitarra;** I know how to do it, **yo sé hacerlo;** to know (to be acquainted with a person, place), **conocer;** I know Robert, **yo conozco a Roberto;** I know Madrid, **yo conozco Madrid**

L

la *def. art., f., s.,* the; **la chica,** the girl; *pl.,* **las chicas**

lamp, **la lámpara**

language, **la lengua**

lápiz *n.m.,* pencil; *pl.,* **los lápices**

large *adj.,* **gran, grande;** a large book, **un gran libro;** a large house, **una casa grande;** a large building, **un edificio grande**

---

lástima *n.f.*, pity; **¡qué lastima!** what a pity! what a shame!

late *adv.*, **tarde;** later, **más tarde**

laugh *v.*, **reír;** see **reír** among the 22 verbs in the Appendix

learn *v.*, **aprender**

leave *v.*, **partir, salir;** I am leaving, **parto, salgo;** to leave the house, **salir de casa**

leche *n.f.*, milk

leer *v.*, to read; see **leer** among the 22 verbs in the Appendix

left (as opposed to *right*) **izquierda; a la izquierda,** to (on, at) the left; see Antonyms in the Appendix

lengua *n.f.*, language; tongue

letter, **la carta**

lettuce, **la lechuga**

levantarse *refl. v.*, to get up; **¿a qué hora se levanta Ud.?** at what time do you get up?

libro *n.m.*, book

like *v.*, **gustar;** I like ice cream, **me gusta el helado;** I like to write, **me gusta escribir**

little (not much in quantity) *adv., adj.* **poco, poca, pocos, pocas;** little (in size), **pequeño, pequeña, pequeños, pequeñas**

live *v.*, **vivir;** see **vivir** among the 22 verbs in the Appendix

llamar *v.*, to call; they called, **llamaron; llamarse** *refl. v.* to be named, to be called; **¿cómo se llama Ud.?** or **¿cómo te llamas?** *(fam. form)* what is your name? see **llamarse** among the 22 verbs in the Appendix

llegar *v.*, to arrive

llover *v.*, to rain; it's raining, **llueve** *or* **está lloviendo**

look (at) *v.*, **mirar;** to look for, **buscar**

love *v.*, **amar;** I love you, **yo te amo;** love, **el amor;** to be in love, **estar enamorado(a);** they are in love, **están enamorados**

lunch, **el almuerzo;** to lunch, to have lunch, **almorzar**

lunes *n.m.*, Monday

mal *adv.*, badly; *n.m.*, evil, grief, misfortune

man, **el hombre**

mañana *n.f.*, morning; *adv.*, tomorrow; **todas las mañanas,** every morning

mano *n.f.*, hand

mar *n., f., m.*, sea

March, **marzo** *n.m.*

más *adv.*, more

mashed potatoes, **el puré de patatas**

May, **mayo** *n.m.*

meal, **la comida**

medicamento *n.m.*, medicine (that you take)

mejor *adj., adv.*, better, best

mencionar *v.*, to mention

mi, mis *poss. adj.*, my

mientras *conj.*, while

milk, **la leche**

modern *adj.*, **moderno, moderna, modernos, modernas**

moho *n.m.*, moss

momento *n.m.*, moment; **en este momento,** at this moment

monkey, **el mono**

monster, **el monstruo**

month, **el mes**

morning, **la mañana;** in the morning, **por la mañana;** every morning, **todas las mañanas**

mother, **la madre**

mountain, **la montaña**

moustache, **un bigote, un mostacho**

movediza *adj.*, rolling, moving

movies (cinema), **el cine;** I'm going to the movies, **voy al cine**

much *adj.*, **mucho, mucha, muchos, muchas;** see Antonyms in the Appendix

muchacho *n.m.*, boy

muchas gracias, thank you very much

museo *n.m.*, museum

música *n.f.*, music

muy *adv.*, very; **María es muy simpática,** Mary is very nice; **Juan es muy simpático,** John is very nice

my *poss. adj.*, **mi, mis;** my friend, **mi amigo (amiga);** my friends, **mis amigos (amigas)**

M

madre *n.f.*, mother

maestro *n.m.*, master; teacher, **el maestro, la maestra**

magazine, **la revista**

mail, **el correo**

make *v.*, **hacer;** see the 22 verbs in the Appendix

N

nada *pron.*, nothing, not anything

name, **el nombre**

napkin, **la servilleta**

necesitar *v.*, to need

neither *conj.*, **ni, tampoco**

nevar *v.*, to snow; **está nevando** *or* **nieva,** it's snowing

never *adv.*, **nunca**

new *adj.*, **nuevo, nueva, nuevos, nuevas;** a new overcoat, **un nuevo abrigo;** a new dress, **un nuevo vestido;** a new shirt, **una nueva camisa**

next Saturday, **el sábado que viene**

ni *conj.*, neither

nice *adj.*, **simpático(a);** Helen is nice, **Elena es simpática;** Paul is nice, **Pablo es simpático**

nieve *n.f.*, snow; **me gusta la nieve,** I like snow

night, **la noche;** good-night, good evening, **buenas noches;** every night, **todas las noches**

nine, **nueve;** it's 9 o'clock, **son las nueve;** at 9 o'clock, **a las nueve;** see Numbers in the Appendix

niña *n.f.*, **niño** *n.m.*, child; **los niños** the children

no *adv.*, **no**

nobody, no one *pron.*, **nadie**

noche *n.f.*, night, evening; see *night* in this list

nombrar *v.*, to name; **el nombre,** name

nothing *pron.*, **nada;** I see nothing, **no veo nada**

November, **noviembre** *n.m.*

novicio *n.m.*, novice, beginner

now *adv.*, **ahora**

nueces *n.f.*, *pl.*, walnuts, nuts; *sing.*, **la nuez**

nueve, nine; see Numbers in the Appendix

número *n.m.*, number

nunca *adv.*, never

O

o *conj.*, or

October, **octubre** *n.m.*

of *prep.*, **de**

office, **la oficina**

often *adv.*, **muchas veces, a menudo**

ojo *n.m.*, eye

okay, **de acuerdo, está bien**

opera, **la ópera**

open *v.*, **abrir**

or *conj.*, **o**

orange juice, **el jugo de naranja**

otoño *n.m.*, autumn, fall

overcoat, **el abrigo**

P

padre *n.m.*, father

pagar *v.*, to pay (for); see the 22 verbs in the Appendix

pájaro *n.m.*, bird

pan *n.m.*, bread

pan, **la cacerola, la cazuela;** see *pots and pans* in this list

panadería *n.f.*, bakery shop

papel *n.m.*, paper (writing)

papelería *n.f.*, stationery shop

par *n.m.*, pair, couple; **de par en par,** wide open

para *prep.*, for, in order to; **¿para qué?** what for? for what?

párpados *n.m.*, *pl.*, eyelids

parque *n.m.*, park

party, **la fiesta**

pasar *v.*, to pass, to happen, to spend (time); **pasar un buen rato,** to have a good time

pastelería *n.f.*, pastry shop; pastry, **el pastel, los pasteles**

pay *v.*, **pagar;** see the 22 verbs in the Appendix

peas, **los guisantes**

pen, **la pluma**

pena *n.f.*, pain, penalty, punishment

pensar *v.*, to think; **yo pienso,** I think

pensive *adj.*, **pensativo, pensativa**

pepper, **la pimienta**

pequeño *adj.*, small, little (in size); see Antonyms and Synonyms in the Appendix

pera *n.f.*, pear

pero *conj.*, but

persona *n.f.*, person

peseta *n.f.*, peseta (monetary unit)

pharmacy, **la farmacia**

piano, **el piano**

pie *n.m.*, foot; **ir a pie,** to walk; see **ir** among the 22 verbs in the Appendix

piedra *n.f.*, stone

plane (airplane), **un avión;** air mail, **el correo aéreo**

play *v.*, **jugar;** to play tennis, **jugar al tenis;** to play ball, **jugar a la pelota;** to play the piano, guitar, **tocar el piano, la guitarra**

playa *n.f.*, beach

plaza *n.f.*, plaza, square

pleasant *adj.*, **agradable**

please, **por favor**

pluma *n.f.*, pen

plumbing, **la fontanería** (fixtures); **la plomería**

poco, poca, pocos, pocas *adj.*, little (not much in quantity), few, not much

police, **la policía**

pollo *n.m.*, chicken

por *prep.*, by; **por favor**, please; **¿por qué?** why?
pork chops, **las chuletas de cerdo**
porque *conj.*, because
potato, **la patata, la papa**
pots and pans (kitchen), **la batería de cocina;** pot, **una olla, una marmita;** pan, casserole, **una cacerola, una cazuela**
precio *n.m.*, price
prefer *v.*, **preferir;** I prefer, **yo prefiero**
prepare *v.*, **preparar**
pretty *adj.*, **lindo, linda, lindos, lindas; bonito, bonita, bonitos, bonitas**
price, **el precio;** what is the price? **¿cuál es el precio?**
primavera *n.f.*, spring (season of the year)

repetir *v.*, to repeat; see the 22 verbs in the Appendix
reply *v.*, **contestar, responder**
reside *v.*, **habitar**
respond *v.*, **responder, contestar**
respuesta *n.f.*, answer, reply
revista *n.f.*, magazine
rey *n.m.*, king; **los reyes,** kings, king and queen
rice, **el arroz**
right (as opposed to *left*), **la derecha;** to (on, at) the right, **a la derecha;** to be right, **tener razón;** I am right, **tengo razón;** see the verb **tener** and the review of basic Spanish idioms with **tener** in the Appendix
rolls (bread), **los panecillos, los bollos**
ruido *n.m.*, noise
run *v.*, **correr;** they are running, **ellos corren**

Q

que *conj.* that, than; **yo soy más grande que Juan,** I am taller than John; *adj.* what, which; **yo sé que tú eres inteligente,** I know that you are intelligent; **¿qué postre quiere Ud.?** what (which) dessert do you want? **¿qué tal?** how are things?
quedarse *refl. v.*, to remain, to stay
querer *v.*, to want; see the 22 verbs in the Appendix
querido, querida *adj.*, dear
quien *pron.*, who, whom

R

radiator, **el radiador**
rain *v.*, **llover;** it's raining, **llueve** or **está lloviendo**
ratón *n.m.*, mouse; **los ratones,** mice
read *v.*, **leer;** see the 22 verbs in the Appendix
recibir *v.*, to receive
red *adj.*, **rojo;** a red dress, **un vestido rojo;** a red shirt, **una camisa roja**
reducción *n.f.*, reduction; **reducido** *adj.*, reduced
refrán *n.m.*, proverb, saying
refuse *v.*, **rehusar**
regla *n.f.*, rule, ruler
reír *v.*, to laugh; see the 22 verbs in the Appendix
relative (person), **el pariente**
remain *v.*, **quedarse** *refl. v.*

S

sábado *n.m.*, Saturday; **el sábado que viene,** next Saturday
saber *v.*, to know (how); **yo sé nadar,** I know how to swim; **yo sé que tú eres simpático(a),** I know that you are nice; **yo sé escribir en español,** I know how to write in Spanish
saleslady, **la vendedora;** salesman, **el vendedor**
salir *v.*, to leave; **salgo a las tres,** I'm leaving at 3 o'clock
salt, **la sal**
sand, **la arena**
Saturday, **el sábado;** next Saturday, **el sábado que viene**
say *v.*, **decir;** see the 22 verbs in the Appendix
school, **la escuela**
se *refl. pron.*, himself, herself, oneself, itself, themselves; **Elena se lava,** Helen is washing (herself); **ellos se lavan,** they are washing (themselves)
search (for) *v.*, **buscar;** he is searching for (looking for) his necktie, **él busca su corbata**
sed *n.f.*, thirst; **tengo sed,** I am thirsty
see *v.*, **ver;** I see my friends, **veo a mis amigos;** I saw a Spanish movie, **yo vi una película española**
seis, six; **a las seis,** at six o'clock; **son las seis,** it is six o'clock; see Numbers in the Appendix
semana *n.f.*, week
señor *n.m.*, sir, mister; **señora** *n.f.*, madam, Mrs., woman
señorita *n.f.*, Miss

sentir(se) *v.*, to feel (health); **¿tú te sientes mejor?** do you feel better? **sí, yo me siento mejor ahora** yes, I feel better now

September, **septiembre** *n.m.*

ser *v.*, to be; see basic Spanish idioms with **ser** and the 22 verbs in the Appendix

servicio *n.m.*, service

she *pron.*, **ella;** she is writing a letter, **ella escribe una carta**

ship, **un paquebote, un vapor**

shirt, **la camisa**

shoes, **los zapatos**

shop *v.*, **ir de compras;** I'm going shopping, **voy de compras;** shopping bag, **un saco;** see the verb **ir** among the 22 verbs in the Appendix

shopping center, **el centro comercial**

short *adj.*, **corto, pequeño**

si *conj.*, if

sí, yes

sick *adj.*, **enfermo(a);** to be sick, **estar enfermo;** see the review of basic Spanish idioms with **estar** and the 22 verbs in the Appendix

sidewalk, **la acera**

siempre *adv.*, always; See Antonyms in the Appendix

sing *v.*, **cantar**

sister, **la hermana**

situado *adj.*, situated, located

six, **seis;** at six o'clock, **a las seis;** it is six o'clock, **son las seis;** see Numbers in the Appendix

skirt, **la falda**

sleep *v.*, **dormir;** I sleep very well, **yo duermo muy bien**

snow *v.*, **nevar; nieva** *or* **está nevando,** it's snowing; *n.*, **la nieve;** I like snow, **me gusta la nieve**

soap, **el jabón**

socio *n.m.*, socia *n.f.*, member (of a club)

soiled *adj.*, **sucio(a)**

somebody, someone *pron.*, **alguien**

something *pron.*, **algo**

son, **el hijo**

sorry, I'm, **lo siento**

Spanish (language), **el español**

speak *v.*, **hablar;** see the 22 verbs in the Appendix

spectators, **los espectadores**

spring (season of the year), **la primavera**

Sr., *abbreviation for* **señor; Sra.,** *abbreviation for* **señora; Srta.,** *abbreviation for* **señorita**

stage (in a theater), **la escena**

station, **la estación**

stay *v.*, **quedarse** *refl. v.*

store, **la tienda;** department store, **el almacén**

strawberry, **la fresa;** fresh strawberries, **fresas frescas**

street, **la calle**

string beans, **las habichuelas tiernas**

strong *adj.*, **fuerte;** see Antonyms in the Appendix

student, **el (la) estudiante, el alumno, la alumna**

stupid *adj.*, **estúpido(a), tonto(a)**

su *poss. adj.*, your, his, her, their; **su nombre,** your name

sugar, **el azúcar**

suit, **el traje**

suitcase, **la maleta**

summer, **el verano**

sun, **el sol**

sweater, **un suéter;** he is wearing a sweater, **él lleva un suéter**

swim *v.*, **nadar;** I like to swim, **me gusta nadar;** swim suit, **el traje de baño**

T

tablecloth, **el mantel**

take *v.*, **tomar;** to take a sun bath, **tomar el sol;** to take a trip, **hacer un viaje;** see the basic Spanish idioms with **hacer** and the 22 verbs in the Appendix

tal *adj.*, such; **tal padre, tal hijo,** like father, like son; **¿qué tal?** how are things? what's up?

talk *v.*, **hablar;** see the 22 verbs in the Appendix

tall *adj.*, **alto, alta, altos, altas**

también *adv.*, also, too

tarde *n.f.*, afternoon; **buenas tardes,** good afternoon; *adv.*, late; **es tarde,** it is late

taxi, **el taxi**

tea, **el té**

teach *v.*, **enseñar**

telefonear *v.*, to telephone; see the 22 verbs in the Appendix

teléfono *n.m.*, telephone

tell *v.*, **decir;** see the 22 verbs in the Appendix

temprano *adv.*, early

tener *v.*, to have, to hold; see the review of basic Spanish idioms with **tener** and the 22 verbs in the Appendix

thank you very much, **muchas gracias**

theater, **el teatro**

there are, there is, **hay**

they *pron., m. & m.f., pl.*, **ellos;** *f., pl.* **ellas**

thing, **la cosa**

thirst, **la sed;** I am thirsty, **tengo sed**

thirty, **treinta;** see Numbers in the Appendix

this *demons. adj.,* **este, esta;** this day, **este día;** this book, **este libro;** this skirt, **esta falda;** this evening (tonight), **esta noche**

ticket, **el billete, el boleto**

time, **la hora;** what time is it? **¿qué hora es?** time in general, **el tiempo;** I don't have much time because I'm going to Spanish class, **no tengo mucho tiempo porque voy a la clase de español; el tiempo** also means weather; what's the weather like? **¿qué tiempo hace?**

to *prep.,* **a;** to the movies (cinema), **al cine;** to church, **a la iglesia;** to school, **a la escuela;** to the supermarket, **al supermercado;** to the boys, **a los muchachos;** to the girls, **a las muchachas**

toast, **el tostado, el pan tostado**

tocar *v.,* to play (a musical instrument); **toco la guitarra,** I play the guitar

todas las noches, every night (evening)

today *adv.,* **hoy**

todo, toda, todos, todas *adj.,* all; **todas las mañanas,** every morning; **todos los días,** every day

tomar *v.,* to take, to have (something to eat or drink); **yo voy a tomar un café con crema,** I'm going to have a coffee with cream; **yo tomo leche,** I'm having milk; **tome este medicamento,** take this medicine

tomato, **el tomate**

tomorrow *adv.,* **mañana**

too (also) *adv.,* **también**

towel, **la toalla**

trabajar *v.,* to work

traducir *v.,* to translate; **tradúzcalos,** translate them

traer *v.,* to bring

train, **el tren**

traje *pret., 1st pers., sing. of* **traer; yo traje el helado,** I brought the ice cream; *n.m.,* suit

travel *v.,* **viajar**

tres, three; see Numbers in the Appendix

trip, **un viaje;** to take (go on) a trip, **hacer un viaje;** see the basic review of Spanish idioms with **hacer** and the 22 verbs in the Appendix

trousers, **los pantalones**

tú *pron., 2nd pers., sing.,* you; **¿tú ves?** do you see?

tu *poss. adj.,* your; **tu tío,** your uncle; **tu amiga,** your girlfriend; **tu amigo,** your boyfriend

twenty, **veinte;** two, **dos;** see Numbers in the Appendix

U

Ud. (usted) *s.,* **Uds. (ustedes)** *pl., pron.,* you; also **Vd., Vds.**

ugly *adj.,* **feo, fea, feos, feas**

un, uno, una, one; **un libro,** one (a) book; **uno de los muchachos,** one of the boys; **una de las muchachas,** one of the girls; see Numbers in the Appendix

uncle, **et tío**

United States, **los Estados Unidos;** U.S., **EE. UU.**

until *adv.,* **hasta**

V

vacation, **las vacaciones;** to go on vacation, **ir de vacaciones**

valedero *adj.,* valid

valer *v.,* to be worth

valise, **la maleta**

vase, **el jarrón**

Vd. Vds., see **Ud., Uds.**

vegetables, **las legumbres**

veinte, twenty; see Numbers in the Appendix

vender *v.,* to sell

ver *v.,* to see; **¿tú ves?** do you see?

verano *n.m.,* summer

very *adv.,* **muy**

viajar *v.,* to travel; **hacer un viaje,** to take (go on) a trip; see the basic review of Spanish idioms with **hacer** and the 22 verbs in the Appendix

vino *n.m.,* wine

violin, **el violín**

vista *n.f.* view; **buena vista,** good view

vivir *v.,* to live, to reside

volando, flying

volar *v.,* to fly

W

waiter, **el mesero;** waitress, **la mesera**

walk *v.* **andar, ir a pie;** he (she) is walking, **él (ella) anda;** to take a walk, **dar un paseo;** I'm taking a walk through the park, **doy un paseo por el parque;** see **ir** and **dar** among the 22 verbs in the Appendix

want *v.,* **querer;** see the 22 verbs in the Appendix

watch television, **mirar la televisión (la tele)**

weak *adj.*, **débil;** see Antonyms in the Appendix

wear *v.*, **llevar;** he is wearing a sweater, **él lleva un suéter**

weather, **el tiempo;** what's the weather like? **¿qué tiempo hace?** the weather is pleasant, **hace un tiempo agradable**

week, **la semana**

well *adv.*, **bien**

what do you want? **¿qué desea Ud.? ¿qué quiere Ud.?**

what is the address? **¿cuál es la dirección?**

what is the date? **¿cuál es la fecha?**

what is this? **¿qué es esto?**

what is your name? **¿cuál es su nombre?** or **¿cómo se llama Ud.?**

what time is it? **¿qué hora es?**

what's the weather like in summer? **¿qué tiempo hace en el verano?** see the review of basic Spanish idioms with **hacer** and the 22 verbs in the Appendix

when *conj., adv.*, **cuando**

where *adv.*, **donde**

which cinema? **¿qué cine?** see **que** in this list for difference between **que** and **qué**

who, whom *pron.*, **quien**

who is it? **¿quién es?**

why *adv.*, **por qué**

wife, **la esposa**

window, **la ventana**

wine, **el vino**

winter, **el invierno**

with *prep.*, **con;** with me, **conmigo, conmiga**

woman, **la mujer, la dama, la señora**

work *v.*, **trabajar;** *n.*, **el trabajo**

worried *adj.*, **inquieto, inquieta**

write *v.*, **escribir;** see the 22 verbs in the Appendix

wrong, to be *v.*, **no tener razón;** see the review of basic Spanish idioms with **tener** and the verb **tener** among the 22 verbs in the Appendix

Y

y *conj.*, and; see the entry *and* in this list

year, **el año**

yes *adv.*, **sí**

yesterday *adv.*, **ayer**

yo *pron.*, I

you *pron.*, **tú** *(2nd pers., sing., familiar form)*, **Ud.** or **Vd. (usted)** *polite form, sing.*, **Uds. or Vds. (ustedes)** *polite form, pl.*

Answers

NOTE TO USERS OF THIS BOOK. Exercise I in the 40 Tareas contains words, phrases, and idiomatic expressions related in thought in Spanish with English equivalents. The model sentences in Exercise I illustrate their use. Students are requested to write their own sentences, imitating the models in Spanish. Therefore, what students will write in Spanish will vary greatly. For that reason, there are no sample sentences given here for Exercise I in the 40 Tareas. The model sentences in Spanish may be used to copy on the lines for practice if students are not yet able to write simple sentences of their own. Then they can compare what they wrote in Spanish with the model sentences.

TAREA 1
II. 1. llamo 2. años 3. levanto 4. mañanas 5. da **III.** 1. Me llamo (plus your name). 2. Tengo (number) años. 3. Me levanto a las seis. **IV.** Me llamo Roberto (Roberta). Tengo diez y siete años. Todas las mañanas me levanto a las seis. **V.** El muchacho bebe leche. **VI.** hoy **VII.** ahora **VIII.** 1. leche 2. pan 3. cereal **IX.** 1. yo 2. de 3. uno **X.** 1. Yo me levanto. 2. Yo tomo un buen desayuno.

TAREA 2
II. 1. calor 2. frío 3. tiempo 4. fresco 5. agradable **III.** Hace calor en el verano. 2. Hace frío en el invierno. 3. Hace buen tiempo en la primavera. 4. Hace fresco aquí en el otoño. 5. Hace un tiempo agradable hoy. Voy al parque. **IV.** En el otoño hace fresco. Hace frío en el invierno. Hace buen tiempo en la primavera. Hace calor en el verano. Hoy hace un tiempo agradable. Voy al parque. **V.** La muchacha baila. **VI.** buen **VII.** perro **VIII.** 1. hace 2. calor 3. frío 4. fresco 5. agradable 6. tiempo **IX.** 1. la 2. el 3. da 4. de 5. al 6. del **X.** hace

TAREA 3
II. 1. llueve 2. nieva 3. doy 4. en 5. hay **III.** 1. Leo un libro en mi dormitorio. 2. Voy al parque. 3. Doy un paseo en el parque. 4. Leo los periódicos en casa. 5. Las estaciones del año son la primavera, el verano, el otoño, el invierno. **IV.** Cuando llueve leo un libro en mi dormitorio. Cuando nieva voy al parque. Doy un paseo en el parque. **V.** El muchacho lee un libro. **VI.** casa **VII.** porque **VIII.** 1. Yo leo. 2. Yo voy. 3. Yo doy. **IX.** Cuando nieva voy al parque. **X.** leo, mi

REVIEW TEST 1
I. Me llamo (plus your name). Tengo (number) años. Todas las mañanas me levanto a las siete. Tomo un buen desayuno. **II.** Hace calor en el verano. Hace frío en el invierno. Hace buen tiempo en la primavera. Hace fresco en el otoño. **III.** Cuando llueve leo un libro en mi dormitorio. Cuando nieva voy al parque. Doy un paseo en el parque. **IV.** 1. levanto 2. mañanas, buen 3. frío, verano 4. escribir **V.** 1. un libro 2. periódicos 3. leche **VI.** 1. El muchacho lee un libro. 2. La muchacha baila. 3. El muchacho bebe leche. **VII.** casa **VIII.** porque **IX.** 1. Yo leo. 2. Yo voy al parque. 3. Yo doy un paseo en el parque. **X.** 1. la 2. el 3. da 4. de 5. al 6. del

TAREA 4
II. 1. bien 2. estoy 3. mejor 4. al 5. pasar **III.** 1. Estoy enfermo(a). 2. Está bien. 3. Cuando estoy enfermo(a) yo voy al médico. 4. Voy a pasar dos semanas en el campo. 5. Voy al parque. **IV.** 1. Estoy 2. bien 3. enfermo(a) 4. mucho 5. mejor 6. el médico **V.** La chica y el chico corren. **VI.** 1. bien 2. enfermo(a) 3. mejor **VII.** Voy a pasar una semana en el campo. **VIII.** una semana (dos semanas) **IX.** 1. un libro 2. periódicos 3. pasteles **X.** Querido amigo, yo voy a pasar una semana en el campo. Parto mañana. Hasta la vista. **XI.** bien, enfermo(a), diez y siete, todas

TAREA 5

II. 1. de 2. tengo 3. sed 4. comer 5. en **III.** 1. Tengo ganas de beber. 2. Como cuando tengo hambre. 3. Bebo agua cuando tengo sed. 4. Acostumbro comer en casa. 5. Una persona entra en un restaurante para comer. **IV.** 1. No es un sombrero. Es un bizcocho. 2. Sí, es delicioso. **V.** 1. un bizcocho 2. leche 3. pan 4. frutas 5. arroz 6. peras **VI.** 1. Como cuando tengo hambre. 2. Bebo cuando tengo sed. 3. Acostumbro comer en casa. **VII.** Muchas gracias, pero no hoy porque estoy enfermo(a).

TAREA 6

II. 1. gran 2. gusta 3. está 4. jugar 5. pelota **III.** esta, jugar, está, de, al, voy, jugar, pelota **IV.** 1. Hay un gran parque en esta ciudad. 2. Voy al parque cuando hay sol. 3. El parque está cerca de mi casa. 4. Me gusta jugar al tenis en el parque. 5. Hoy yo voy al parque a jugar a la pelota. **V.** Ella está en un parque. Ella juega a la pelota. **VI.** Voy al parque. Voy a jugar a la pelota en el parque. **VII.** voy, jugar, al tenis

REVIEW TEST 2

I. No estoy bien hoy. Voy al campo. Voy a pasar dos semanas en el campo. **II.** Tengo ganas de comer. Como cuando tengo hambre. Bebo agua cuando tengo sed. Acostumbro comer en casa. **III.** Hay un gran parque cerca de mi casa. Voy a pie al parque. Me gusta jugar al tenis y a la pelota en el parque. Voy al parque cuando hay sol. **IV.** 1. La chica y el chico corren. 2. Es un bizcocho. 3. La muchacha juega a la pelota.

TAREA 7

II. 1. es 2. una 3. las 4. qué 5. tres 6. tengo **III.** 1. Es la una (Son las dos, *etc.*). 2. Tomo el desayuno a las siete. 3. Tomo el almuerzo a la una. 4. Tomo la cena a las ocho. 5. Todas las noches me acuesto a las diez. **IV.** la, las, voy, la, de, las, tengo, con, a, y **V.** 1. Son las cuatro. 2. Son las tres y media. **VI.** Voy a la clase de español a las tres. Tengo cita con el dentista a las cuatro. **VII.** 1. Voy a la clase de español a la una. 2. Voy al dentista a las tres. 3. Voy a casa a las cuatro. **VIII.** La fecha: el primero de octubre. La hora: Es la una. La Señora García tiene cita a las tres pero llega a las cuatro. (Su nombre:' Your name).

TAREA 8

II. 1. tiene 2. museo 3. tiene 4. muchos 5. está 6. izquierda **III.** 1. Hay muchas obras de arte. 2. Hay muchos libros. 3. Está a la derecha. 4. Todas las noches me acuesto a las once. 5. Sí. Me gusta escribir en español. **IV.** 1. muchas obras de arte. 2. muchos libros **V.** 1. Cuesta 501 pesetas. 2. de Madrid. 3. Voy a Barcelona. 4. Llego a la estación Norte. 5. en la clase dos. 6. Para dos adultos. Para tres niños. 7. del 22 octubre al 21 de diciembre. 8. No hay una reducción de precio.

TAREA 9

II. 1. a 2. a 3. leer 4. voz 5. baja **III.** 1. Sí. Me gusta leer en español. 2. Le toca a Roberto. 3. Yo sé escribir en español. 4. Hablo en voz baja. 5. Yo almuerzo a la una. **IV.** 1. en voz alta 2. mal 3. a la izquierda 4. estar bien **V.** Yo voy a leer. Sí. Yo sé leer muy bien en español. Hablo en voz alta en la clase de español. **VI.** 1. LEER 2. HABLAR 3. CONTESTO 4. HABLO 5. LEO 6. SIEMPRE **VII.** Es un libro.

REVIEW TEST 3

I. Voy a la clase de español a la una. Tengo cita con el dentista a las dos y media. **II.** Hay muchas obras de arte en un museo. Hay muchos libros en una biblioteca. El museo está a la izquierda. La biblioteca está a la derecha. **III.** Roberto va a leer en inglés. Yo voy a leer en español. Elena va a escribir en inglés. Yo voy a escribir en español. **IV.** 1. Es un libro. 2. Es la una. 3. Son las dos y media. 4. Cuesta 501 pesetas. 5. Salgo de Barcelona. 6. Voy a Madrid. 7. Llego a la estación Goya. 8. Viajo en la clase dos. 9. Este billete es para dos adultos y tres niños. 10. Este billete es valedero del 22 de septiembre al 21 de octubre.

TAREA 10

II. Señorita Margarita Morales, 15 Avenida Goya, 32015 Madrid, España. Fecha: el primero de noviembre. Querida Margarita, ¡Hola! Me llamo (plus your name). Tengo (plus number) años. Me levanto a las seis de la mañana. Todas las mañanas tomo un buen desayuno. Ahora voy a jugar al tenis en el parque porque hace un tiempo agradable. Me gusta mucho jugar a la pelota también. Con cariño, (plus your name). **III.** 1. El sábado que viene pienso ir a España. 2. Sí. Quiero ir a Madrid. Quiero pasearme en automóvil por las calles de Madrid. 3. Bebo leche y como pasteles. 4. Mi mejor amigo(a) se llama Roberto(a). 5. Me gustan las peras, las bananas, y las naranjas (oranges). **IV.** 1. La fecha es lunes, el veinte y dos (veintidós) de noviembre. (Consult the section on Numbers in the back pages of this book). 2. Paula Martínez escribe la carta. 3. Paula Martínez desea recibir un ejemplar de la Revista de Lenguas. 4. Ella aprende inglés, francés, italiano, y alemán. 5. Paula vive en la Calle de las Flores, número doce, en Madrid.

TAREA 11

II. 1. está 2. madre 3. veces 4. vez 5. lado **III.** 1. Cerca de aquí. 2. Mi madre. 3. Trabajo. **IV.** 1. el grifo 2. el radiador 3. la secadora de ropa (Consult the vocabulary in the back pages of this book.) Or, you may write: la fontanería (la plomería), la calefacción, la electricidad. **V.** 1. Es una casa. 2. Es una lámpara.

TAREA 12

II. 1. me 2. de 3. todas 4. visto 5. peino **III.** 1. Sí. Me lavo todas las mañanas. 2. Sí. Me lavo antes de salir de casa. 3. Sí. Me limpio los dientes todas las mañanas. 4. Sí. Me peino todos los días. 5. Me visto en mi dormitorio. **IV. A.** 1. lavarse 2. limpiar(se) 3. peinarse (Consult the section on 109 verbs used in this book in the back pages.) **B.** 1. la madre 2. el chico 3. las manos

REVIEW TEST 4

I. See Answers, Tarea 10, Ex. II. **II.** Mi casa está situada cerca de aquí. Mi madre pone la mesa para las comidas. De vez en cuando yo trabajo en el jardín. Al lado de nuestra casa hay buenos vecinos. **III.** 1. el grifo 2. el radiador 3. la secadora de ropa 4. la lámpara **IV.** 1. semana 2. ir 3. escribo 4. trabajo 5. pone 6. limpio **V.** 1. lavas 2. me 3. limpias 4. las

TAREA 13

II. 1. hacer 2. que 3. hacer 4. acostarme 5. de **III.** 1. Voy a hacer un viaje mañana. 2. a las seis 3. Tengo que hacer las maletas y tengo que hacer los preparativos para el viaje. 4. Porque tengo que levantarme de madrugada. **IV.** 1. Es un tren. 2. Es un barco (un paquebote, un vapor). **V. A.** 1. hacer las maletas. 2. hacer los preparativos **B.** 1. hacer un viaje 2. tener que 3. hacer las maletas **VI.** Mañana voy a hacer un viaje. Tengo que hacer los preparativos para el viaje. Tengo que hacer las maletas, también.

TAREA 14

II. 1. favor 2. no 3. mucho 4. tengo 5. Quítese **III.** 1. Cuando tengo frío, bebo una taza de té caliente (I drink a cup of hot tea). 2. Cuando tengo calor, bebo una limonada. 3. Cuando estoy enfermo(a), voy al médico. 4. Hace frío en el invierno. 5. Hace calor en el verano. **IV.** 1. estar enferma 2. el médico 3. la fiebre 4. la señora

TAREA 15

II. 1. buen 2. de 3. de 4. lo 5. tocar **III.** 1. Gozo de las fiestas. 2. Doy un paseo 3. Porque me gusta el español. 4. Hay siete días. 5. Hay cincuenta y dos semanas. (Consult the section on Numbers in the back pages of this book). **IV.** 1. El hombre da un paseo (El hombre anda). 2. Ella da un paseo (Ella anda). **V.** Gozo de las fiestas los sábados. Doy de comer a los pájaros en el parque. Doy un paseo a lo largo de la playa. Toco el piano. Trabajo. **VI.** 1. no 2. ver 3. ni 4. vino **VII.** 1. parque 2. doy 3. el 4. playa

REVIEW TEST 5

I. 1. Es un barco (un paquebote, un vapor). **II.** Mañana voy a hacer un viaje. Tengo que hacer los preparativos para el viaje. Tengo que hacer las maletas, también. **III.** Cuando tengo frío, bebo una taza de té caliente. Cuando tengo calor, bebo una limonada. Cuando estoy enfermo(a), voy al médico. **IV.** 1. Yo trabajo en un restaurante. 2. Doy un paseo. 3. Toco el piano (la guitarra, *etc.*). **V.** A. 1. hacer las maletas 2. acostarme temprano B. 1. hacer las maletas 2. hacer los preparativos 3. hacer un viaje **VI.** 1. parque 2. doy 3. el 4. playa **VII.** 1. voy 2. que, viaje 3. tengo 4. favor 5. cuarto 6. parque

TAREA 16

II. 1. tarde 2. ejemplo 3. veces 4. centro 5. a **III.** A. 1. el hombre 2. comer 3. mucho 4. el apetito 5. el vino 6. el bizcocho B. 1. cantamos 2. comemos 3. vamos al cine **IV.** 1. Sí. Soy socio del Club Español. 2. Hay quince. 3. hablamos, cantamos, comemos. 4. Mucho ruido y pocas nueces *(Much ado about nothing)*. Tal padre, tal hijo *(Like father, like son)*. There is a proverb (un refrán) in Spanish with an English equivalent at the end of every Review Test.

TAREA 17

II. 1. Miguel 2. tienes 3. dolor 4. siento 5. noche **III.** 1. Tomo una aspirina. 2. Voy a una farmacia. 3. Lo siento mucho. 4. Cincuenta años. 5. Hace frío. **IV.** A. 1. tener buena cara 2. tener dolor de cabeza. B. 1. mala 2. poco 3. noche 4. tarde **V.** Yo no voy a la escuela mañana porque estoy enfermo(a) y tengo dolor de cabeza. Esta noche voy a acostarme temprano. (Don't forget to start your note with either **Querido amigo** or **Querida amiga** and end the note with **Hasta la vista**.)

TAREA 18

II. 1. que 2. mejor 3. español 4. enseña 5. estudiando **III.** 1. la sala de clase 2. el profesor de español 3. tres alumnos 4. corren (correr). 5. Son las tres. 6. ¡Adiós, señor! **IV.** 1. un año (dos años, tres años) 2. Sí. Pienso seguir estudiando español el año próximo. Porque el español es muy fácil. 3. En la clase de español yo estudio, yo leo y escribo.

REVIEW TEST 6

I. A. 1. el hombre 2. comer 3. mucho 4. el apetito 5. el vino 6. el bizcocho B. 1. cantamos 2. comemos 3. vamos al cine **II.** 1. Sí. Yo soy socio del Club Español. 2. Hay once (See the section on Numbers in the back pages of this book.) 3. hablamos, cantamos, comemos, bailamos. **III.** A. 1. tener buena cara 2. tener dolor de cabeza B. 1. mala 2. poco 3. noche 4. tarde **IV.** Querido amigo (Querida amiga), Yo no voy a la escuela mañana porque estoy enfermo(a) y tengo dolor de cabeza. Esta noche voy a acostarme temprano. Hasta la vista (and write your name). **V.** 1. que 2. mejor 3. español 4. enseña 5. estudiando **VI.** 1. hace un año (dos años, tres años) 2. Sí. Pienso seguir estudiando español el año próximo. Me gusta mucho el español. 3. Yo estudio, hablo, leo y escribo en español.

TAREA 19

II. 1. muchas 2. ordinario 3. enfrente 4. amigo(a) 5. tiempo **III.** 1. OFICINA 2. BILLETES 3. QUIEN 4. SIEMPRE **IV.** 1. Sí. Yo voy al cine muchas veces (Voy al cine todos los sábados.) 2. Con mi amigo(a). 3. enfrente de la oficina de correos 4. Mi amigo(a) compra los billetes. 5. las peras, las bananas, las naranjas, las manzanas (apples), y las uvas (grapes) **V.** Yo voy al cine. Está enfrente de la oficina de correos. Voy al cine todos los sábados.

TAREA 20

II. 1. nadie 2. ninguno 3. nuestra (mi) 4. nada 5. nunca **III.** 1. a nadie 2. ningún hermano 3. nada 4. nunca **IV.** 1. NUNCA 2. NADA 3. NADIE **V.** 1. nada 2. nadie 3. nunca 4. algo **VI.** 1. Pablo no habla a nadie. 2. Pablo no tiene amigo ninguno. 3. Pablo ya no viene a mi (nuestra) casa. 4. Pablo no me dice nada. 5. Yo no le hablaré nunca a Pablo.

TAREA 21

II. 1. hora 2. prestar 3. a 4. para 5. a **III.** 1. Comenzamos a escribir en español. 2. papel y lápiz 3. Me gusta el español. 4. Quien canta su mal espanta *(He who sings drives away his grief)*. Más vale pájaro en mano que ciento volando. *(A bird in the hand is worth two in the bush.)* 5. Hace un año (dos años, tres años). **IV.** Ella escribe una carta. **V.** 1. El nombre es Papelería de los Reyes. 2. La dirección es doscientos ochenta y dos, Avenida de los Reyes, Madrid. 3. El número de teléfono es treinta y cuatro, cuarenta y cuatro, veinte y cuatro (veinticuatro), setenta y dos. (In the remaining Tareas and in the Review Tests when you write a number it is good practice to write it out in Spanish words. Consult the section on Numbers in the back pages of this book). 4. Los precios son reducidos. 5. Deseo comprar papel, cuadernos, reglas, plumas, lápices y gomas de borrar.

REVIEW TEST 7

I. De ordinario yo voy al cine todos los sábados. El cine está situado enfrente de la oficina de correos. Mi amigo(a) y yo siempre llegamos al cine a tiempo. **II.** 1. OFICINA 2. BILLETES 3. QUIEN 4. SIEMPRE **III.** Voy al cine. El cine está situado enfrente de la oficina de correos. Voy al cine todos los sábados. **IV.** 1. Pablo no tiene amigo ninguno (Pablo no tiene ningún amigo). 2. Pablo no habla a nadie. 3. Pablo no me dice nada. 4. Pablo ya no viene a nuestra (mi) casa. 5. Yo no le hablaré nunca a Pablo. **V.** Ella escribe una carta. **VI.** 1. El nombre es Papelería de los Reyes. 2. La dirección es doscientos ochenta y dos, Avenida de los Reyes, Madrid. 3. El número de teléfono es treinta y cuatro, cuarenta y cuatro, veinte y cuatro (veinticuatro), setenta y dos. 4. Los precios son reducidos. 5. Deseo comprar papel, cuadernos, reglas, plumas, lápices y gomas de borrar.

TAREA 22

II. 1. de 2. a 3. se 4. ir 5. lugar **III.** 1. Mi padre acaba de salir de casa. 2. Mi padre va a hacer una visita a mi tío. 3. Mi padre se parece mucho a mi tío. 4. Sí. Me gustaría ir con él a la casa de mi tío. 5. No voy a quedarme en casa. Voy con mi padre. **IV.** La fecha (the date): el dos de enero. Querido primo Carlos (Querida prima Carlota), Mi padre acaba de salir de casa. Va a hacer una visita a mi tío. En lugar de quedarme en casa, me gustaría ir con él. ¡Hasta pronto! (Write your name) **V.** 1. ACABAR 2. SALIR 3. HACER 4. PARECER 5. GUSTAR 6. QUEDAR **VI.** 1. es 2. tu (tú) 3. dar 4. día

TAREA 23

II. 1. por 2. de 3. color 4. media 5. me **III.** 1. Yo fui al circo. 2. Estaba de pie sobre una silla. 3. Un zapato era amarillo y el otro verde. 4. El payaso hablaba a un mono. 5. Hablaba a media voz. **IV.** (a) Ayer yo vi un mono. (b) Yo vi el mono en un circo. (c) Yo me reí a carcajadas. (Consult the 22 Spanish verbs fully conjugated in all the tenses in the back pages). **V.** No tiene nada. **VI.** Tú eres un pez. (Note that a fish swimming in water is *un pez*; a fish out of water, caught to be cooked and eaten, is *un pescado*). **VII.** 1. Yo prefiero 2. una película fabulosa 3. muy 4. interesante

TAREA 24

II. 1. quién 2. una 3. está 4. lado 5. buena **III.** 1. Es una corbata. 2. En una tienda. 3. Está por allá. 4. No costó mucho. **IV.** La semana pasada yo compré una pelota. Es roja. Compré la pelota en una tienda. La tienda está cerca de la oficina de correos. No costó mucho y yo pagué de buena gana. **V.** 1. una corbata 2. mi amigo 3. una ganga 4. el precio **VI.** 1. es 2. fue 3. está 4. costó **VII.** 1. ¿de quién . . . ? 2. fue una ganga 3. al otro lado de la calle 4. de buena gana **VIII.** 1. corbatas 2. libros 3. flores 4. frutas **IX.** ganga

REVIEW TEST 8

I. 1. Mi padre 2. a la casa de mi tío 3. a mi tío 4. Sí. Me gustaría ir con mi padre a la casa de mi tío. 5. Voy con él. **II.** La fecha (the date): el catorce de enero. Querido primo Juan (Querida prima Juana), Mi padre acaba de salir de casa. Va a hacer una visita a mi tío. En lugar de quedarme en casa, me gustaría ir con él. ¡ Hasta pronto! (Write your name). **III.** (a) Ayer yo vi un mono. (b) Yo vi el mono en un circo. (c) Yo me reí a carcajadas. **IV.** El muchacho no tiene nada en la mano. **V.** Tú eres un pez. **VI.** 1. Yo prefiero 2. una película fabulosa 3. muy 4. interesante **VII.** 1. una corbata 2. mi amigo 3. una ganga 4. el precio **VIII.** 1. corbatas 2. libros 3. flores 4. frutas

TAREA 25

II. 1. pasada 2. daño 3. rompí 4. bajaba 5. escribir **III.** 1. me caí 2. bajaba 3. puedo 4. escribir **IV.** 1. la semana pasada 2. hacerse daño 3. apenas 4. bajar la escalera **V.** 1. semana 2. caí 3. daño 4. dedo 5. escalera 6. puedo **VI.** 1. hacerse daño 2. romperse 3. bajar la escalera 4. mejor **VII.** La fecha (the date): el tres de febrero. Querido amigo Mario (Querida amiga Elena), La semana pasada me caí por la escalera. Me hice daño. Me rompí un dedo. Apenas puedo escribir ahora. ¡Hasta luego! (Write your name).

TAREA 26

II. 1. a 2. tarde 3. mucha 4. en 5. con **III.** 1. una batería de cocina 2. una oalla 3. una marmita 4. una cacerola **IV.** La fecha: el diez de febrero. Querido amigo Arturo (Querida amiga Elena), Tengo la invitación. Muchas gracias. Yo voy a asistir a la boda con mucho gusto. Tú eres un buen amigo (una buena amiga). ¡Adiós! (Write your name). **V.** 1. Ayer yo asistí a una boda. 2. La ceremonia terminó a las seis en punto.

TAREA 27

II. 1. que 2. de 3. tengo 4. tiene 5. supuesto **III.** 1. el chico y la chica 2. el perro 3. mirar la televisión 4. tener miedo **IV.** ¡Hola! ¿Cómo estás? ¿Qué deseas? ¿Qué cine? No. Tengo miedo de cruzar el parque de noche. Es muy peligroso. Yo prefiero el próximo sábado a las dos de la tarde. De acuerdo. ¡Adiós!

REVIEW TEST 9

I. 1. semana 2. caí 3. daño 4. dedo 5. escalera 6. puedo **II.** 1. hacerse daño 2. romperse 3. bajar la escalera 4. mejor **III.** La fecha: el veinte de febrero. Querido amigo José (Querida amiga María), La semana pasada yo me caí por la escalera. Me hice daño. Me rompí un dedo. Apenas puedo escribir ahora. ¡Hasta luego! (Write your name). **IV.** La fecha: el primero de marzo. Querido amigo Alberto (Querida amiga Ana), Tengo la invitación. Muchas gracias. Yo voy a asistir a la boda con mucho gusto. Tú eres un buen amigo (una buena amiga). Adiós (Write your name). **V.** ¡Hola! ¿Cómo estás? ¿Qué deseas? ¿Qué cine? No. Tengo miedo de cruzar el parque de noche. Es muy peligroso. Yo prefiero el próximo sábado a las tres de la tarde. De acuerdo. ¡Adiós!

TAREA 28

II. 1. en 2. todo 3. estaba 4. descansé 5. siento **III.** 1. el vestido 2. los pantalones 3. el armario 4. estar 5. contenta 6. pensar **IV.** (a) El sábado yo trabajé todo el día. (b) El domingo descansé. (c) Ahora me siento muy bien. **V.** 1. trabajar 2. mucho 3. restaurante fast-food 4. descansar

TAREA 29

II. 1. pasó 2. fui 3. es 4. el 5. me **III.** La fecha: el quince de marzo. Querido amigo Jesús (Querida amiga Teresa), ¡Oh! ¡Dios mío! ¡Eso es una lástima! ¿Herido(a) en un accidente de coche? Lo siento mucho. ¿Tú estás mejor ahora? Es necesario tener esperanza. ¡El tiempo da buen consejo! ¡Quien canta su mal espanta! ¡Adiós! (Write your name). (Consult the index of idioms, verbal expressions, proverbs and key words showing their location in this book). **IV.** ¡Hola, Teresa! No estoy bien porque fui herida en un accidente. En un accidente de coche. ¡Todo el mundo me hace la misma pregunta! No es grave. Me encuentro mejor ahora. Gracias, Teresa.

TAREA 30

II. 1. a 2. principio 3. veinte 4. fui 5. falta **III.** Le pedí dinero a mi madre. Mi madre me dio treinta dólares. Yo fui de compras. Yo compré zapatos. **IV.** A. 1. la señorita 2. ir de compras 3. pagar 4. dinero B. 1. un abrigo bonito 2. un vestido lindo 3. botas 4. revistas y libros **V.** 1. lechuga 2. tomates 3. pan 4. jamón 5. queso 6. frutas

REVIEW TEST 10

I. 1. el armario 2. la ropa 3. estar 4. contenta 5. el marido 6. pensar **II.** La fecha: el primero de abril. Querido amigo Edmundo (Querida amiga Clara), ¡Oh! ¡Dios mío! ¿Herido(a) en un accidente de coche? ¡Eso es una lástima! Lo siento mucho. ¿Tú estás mejor ahora? Es necesario tener esperanza. ¡El tiempo da buen consejo! ¡Quien canta su mal espanta! ¡Adiós! (Write your name). **III.** A. 1. ir de compras 2. la señorita 3. pagar 4. una ganga B. 1. un abrigo bonito 2. un vestido lindo 3. botas 4. libros y revistas **IV.** 1. lechuga 2. tomates 3. pan 4. jamón 5. queso 6. frutas

TAREA 31

II. 1. cincuenta (cuarenta, *etc.*) 2. a 3. todas 4. dio 5. a **III.** El hombre es mi tío. Hoy es cocinero. Ahora está en la cocina. Prepara una comida para toda la familia. Tenemos una fiesta para mi padre. Cumplió cincuenta años. La comida que mi tío prepara es un regalo para mi padre. Quiero mucho a mi tío y a mi padre. Son buenos hombres. **IV.** La fecha: el cinco de abril. Querida Cristina (Querido Manuel), Muchas gracias por la invitación a la fiesta en tu casa. ¿Qué regalo deseas? Lo siento mucho, pero no es posible ir a tu casa porque me hice daño. La semana pasada me caí por la escalera y me rompí un dedo. Es necesario quedarme en casa porque tengo la fiebre también. ¡Hasta la vista! (Write your name).

TAREA 32

II. 1. salió 2. de 3. se 4. se 5. eran **III.** 1. una señora 2. delante de una panadería 3. Se pusieron a hablar. 4. Se vende pan. 5. pasteles **IV. A.** 1. salir de 2. detenerse 3. acercarse 4. ponerse a **B.** 1. pan 2. panecillos **V. A.** Deseo pan y panecillos, por favor. **B.** Perdóneme, por favor, señor. ¿Dónde está una panadería? **C.** Perdóneme, por favor, con permiso. Me gustaría un pastel. Muchas gracias. **VI.** 1. arroz con pollo 2. pasteles

TAREA 33

II. 1. se 2. repente 3. se 4. seguida 5. instante **III.** 1. la chica 2. la madre 3. Porque la chica se puso el nuevo sombrero de su madre. 4. la chica 5. Puso el sombrero en el cajón. **IV. A.** 1. ponerse 2. enfadarse 3. entró 4. empezó **B.** 1. de repente 2. en seguida 3. al instante **V. A.** Me gustaría comprar un vestido. **B.** Me gustaría comprar una camisa. **C.** Muchas gracias, señor (señora, señorita). ¡Usted es magnífico(a)! **VI.** 1. madre

REVIEW TEST 11

I. El hombre es mi tío. Hoy es cocinero. Ahora está en la cocina. Prepara una comida para toda la familia. Tenemos una fiesta para mi padre. Cumplió cincuenta años. La comida que mi tío prepara es un regalo para mi padre. Quiero mucho a mi tío y a mi padre. Son buenos hombres. **II.** La fecha: el veinte de abril. Querida Rosa (Querido Luis), Muchas gracias por la invitación a la fiesta en tu casa. ¿Qué regalo deseas? Lo siento mucho, pero no es posible ir a tu casa porque me hice daño. La semana pasada me caí por la escalera y me rompí los dos pies. Es necesario quedarme en casa porque tengo la fiebre también. ¡Hasta luego! (Write your name). **III. A.** Deseo pan y panecillos, por favor. **B.** Perdóneme, por favor, con permiso, señor. ¿Dónde está una panadería? **C.** Perdóneme, por favor, con permiso. Me gustaría un pastel. Muchas gracias, señor (señora, señorita). **IV. A.** Me gustaría comprar un vestido. **B.** Me gustaría comprar una corbata y una camisa. **C.** Muchas gracias, señor (señora, señorita). ¡Usted es fabuloso(a)!

TAREA 34

II. 1. a 2. vez 3. gusta 4. de 5. vista **III.** 1. en la escuela 2. a la ópera 3. Yo toco la guitarra (el piano, *etc.*) **IV. A.** 1. a la ópera 2. al teatro **B.** 1. el actor 2. en una ópera 3. en un teatro 4. magnífico **V.** La fecha: el primero de mayo. Querida Susana (Querido Marcelo), He conocido a mucha gente aquí en Málaga. Anoche fui a la ópera. A propósito, ¿te gusta la ópera? No te olvides de escribirme. ¡Adiós! (Write your name).

TAREA 35

II. 1. en 2. tiempo 3. de 4. de 5. de **III.** 1. Pienso en mis tareas. 2. Pienso en mi mejor amigo(a). 3. (a) Piedra movediza, el moho no la cobija. (b) Mientras hay alma hay esperanza. (c) Si a Roma fueres, haz como vieres. **IV.** 1. ir de camping o ir a la playa **V.** 1. inteligente 2. extraordinario 3. grave 4. pequeño **VI.** 1. ser 2. par 3. pera 4. pena 5. se 6. en

TAREA 36

II. 1. bastante 2. de 3. semana 4. menos 5. para **III.** 1. El apartamento está situado en Madrid. 2. Hay dos dormitorios. 3. Hay dos baños. 4. Es grande. 5. Se llama El Retiro. 6. Se llama el Museo del Prado. 7. Es treinta y cuatro, cincuenta y cuatro, treinta y dos, sesenta y nueve. **IV. A.** 1. la tarjeta de embarque 2. el vuelo 3. el equipaje 4. la hora de embarco 5. la fecha 6. la fila—el asiento

I. La fecha: el cuatro de mayo. Querida Sara (Querido Marcos), He conocido a mucha gente aquí en Málaga. Anoche fui a la ópera. A propósito, ¿te gusta la ópera? No te olvides de escribirme. ¡Adiós! (Write your name). **II.** 1. Yo pienso en mis tareas. 2. Pienso en mi mejor amigo(a). 3. (a) Tal padre, tal hijo. (b) Dicho y hecho (located at the end of Review Test 2). (c) Más vale tarde que nunca (located at the end of Review Test 3). **III.** 1. bastante (muy). 2. de 3. semana 4. menos 5. para **IV.** 1. Está situado en Madrid. 2. Hay dos dormitorios. 3. Hay dos baños. 4. Es grande. 5. Se llama El Retiro. 6. Se llama el Museo del Prado. 7. Es treinta y cuatro, cincuenta y cuatro, treinta y dos, sesenta y nueve.

TAREA 37

II. 1. de 2. iré 3. iré 4. con 5. hacer **III.** 1. hacer la maleta 2. ir a Madrid 3. pasar dos semanas 4. visitar 5. el Museo del Prado 6. el gran parque, El Retiro **IV.** 1. nadar 2. me gusta 3. la playa 4. jugar **V.** 1. me gustaría 2. comprar 3. ir de vacaciones 4. el verano

TAREA 38

II. 1. eso 2. poco 3. media 4. de 5. llamó

III.

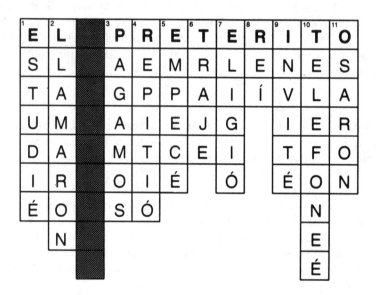

IV. A. 1. yo estudié 2. yo llamé 3. yo hablé 4. yo aprendí 5. yo hice 6. yo reí **B.** 1. nosotros hablamos 2. nosotros escribimos 3. nosotros leímos **C.** 1. arroz 2. pollo 3. bizcocho 4. leche

TAREA 39

II. 1. ser 2. a 3. mucho 4. lo 5. dice **III.** 1. trabajar 2. la oficina 3. tarde 4. correr 5. una taza de café 6. olvidar(se) 7. tomar 8. el autobús

TAREA 40

II. 1. dice 2. dice 3. quiere 4. gracias 5. nada **III.** Elena y José hablan por teléfono. Elena dice, "Yo te amo, José." José dice, "Yo te amo también, Elena." Elena va a casarse con José y yo voy a asistir a la boda.

REVIEW TEST 13

I. 1. hacer la maleta 2. ir a Madrid 3. pasar dos semanas 4. visitar 5. el Museo del Prado 6. el gran parque, El Retiro **II.** 1. nadar 2. me gusta 3. la playa 4. jugar **III. A.** 1. yo estudié 2. yo llamé 3. yo hablé 4. yo aprendí 5. yo hice 6. yo reí **B.** 1. nosotros hablamos 2. nosotros escribimos 3. nosotros leímos **C.** 1. arroz 2. pollo 3. bizcocho 4. leche **IV.** 1. me gustaría 2. comprar 3. ir de vacaciones 4. el verano